DICK SUTPHEN'S
HYPNOSIS

DICK SUTPHEN'S

HYPNOSIS

ROBERTA SUTPHEN

MEDIA

Published 2023 by Gildan Media LLC
aka G&D Media
www.GandDmedia.com

Front cover design by David Rheinhardt of Pyrographx

Designed by Meghan Day Healey of Story Horse, LLC.

Library of Congress Cataloging-in-Publication Data is available upon request

ISBN: 978-1-7225-0653-7

10 9 8 7 6 5 4 3 2 1

In memory of my husband, Richard Charles Sutphen.

He was Dick Sutphen to the world, but to me,
he was my everything.

Contents

Part One
THEORY AND PRINCIPLES

Part Two
SCRIPTS FOR HYPNOSIS SESSIONS

Preface

Dick Sutphen was a master teacher of hypnosis.

From the early days of his Scottsdale Hypnosis Center to his final days of teaching in Sedona, Arizona, Dick generously shared his knowledge and love for all things metaphysical. He turned to Spirit for advice on a daily basis.

His seminars were filled with ways to challenge the participants to find who they really are and become their authentic selves. He was extremely professional and comfortable on stage. He had the best hypnotic voice in the business: no one even comes close. The wisdom he presented and the processes he put participants through came from hours of research and meditation.

The following processes are from Dick's many notes in three-ring binders, which he left with me. They were for his many seminars and classes. If you knew Dick or listened to any of his audio recordings, you can imagine his voice as you read his words.

This work is designed for professional hypnotists. The first part consists of preliminary material, including basic principles, techniques, and suggestions for working both with seminars and individual clients. The second part consists of scripts for specific hypnotic processes. Readers will note considerable repetition and overlap between the different scripts, especially involving the induction and awakening processes. This is intentional. It will enable practitioners to use a single script for each process rather than having to incorporate different elements from different sections of the book.

Part One
THEORY AND PRINCIPLES

The Divine Laws

The hypnotic methods in this book are based on some basic metaphysical principles. Before embarking on a hypnotic session, it would be wise to understand these principles.

You come into this life agreeing on certain fundamental earth laws. You agree that the sky is blue and the grass is green. We accept that gravity is real and that matter equals energy. Objects are solid and you live, consciously, with all the rest of us.

Earth was created for us to live on, and we all agree on this truth. The entire earth reincarnation process has been set up for us to live many different times in order to fully experience and round out our soul's upward spiritual progress. In order for this to work, we all agree to these earthly terms. We could get into the many layers of different vibrational worlds that exist over and on top of our reality, but let's keep this simple. The earth is earth, you and I are humans, and we see our physical reality the same way.

The Law of Divine Order

If you seek to understand the Law of Divine Order, study the balance of nature, for it works very much the same way.

Everything is as it should be, although humankind is far from experiencing its potential of total harmony. There are no accidents. Your energy, translated into thoughts, words, emotions, and deeds, cause all of your experiences. This ensures that you always have the learning opportunities you require to resolve your karma.

It follows that the collective thoughts, words, emotions, and deeds of mankind create the collective environment for us all. If enough people focus their energy upon peace, we will have peace. If the majority of people are filled with anger, we experience war. We are all one, and like the many subpersonalities within you, the dominant traits of humankind (the energy gestalt) will emerge to resolve our group karma.

At one moment, a fundamentalist evangelist preaches fear from a pulpit in West Virginia, while a yoga instructor directs a loving group meditation in Oregon. One is directing the energy of the gestalt into disharmony, the other into harmony. Hopefully, one can cancel out the other. If we can't attain global harmony, maybe we can balance the disharmony. Certainly as growth-oriented individuals, we must not give up, individually or collectively. As always, fear is the problem, and love is the answer.

The Law of Group Consciousness

Every one of us is part of a great energy gestalt and connected on a level of the collective unconscious. Each individual aspect of the gestalt has its own electrical system and its own vibrational frequency and interacts with all other aspects.

Thus we are all electrically connected to one another and to a central point. On a Higher Self or psychic level, it is possible for anyone to tune into anyone else and to draw upon the awareness of the entire gestalt. As with the concept of the hundredth money, mankind takes advancing steps when group consciousness reaches critical mass and new awareness is accepted by the whole.

The Law of Restriction

We cannot create anything higher than our own level of understanding. Thus society can never get any better than the level of humankind as a whole. Our systems for social change usually only add new burdens to already ineffective systems. Time has proven that this approach to a new society doesn't work. Our mistake is in trying to right the wrongs of the world from the outside in. This is working on the effect instead of the cause and is doomed to failure. Instead we must work from the inside out. Every one of us on this planet can incorporate the power of harmonious thinking, which is the only long-term solution to poverty and limitation.

Beliefs

Your beliefs are individual, not a set of collective agreements. Your beliefs depend on factors such as who you are, who raised you, where you were raised, and your social and economic upbringing.

The first step to manifesting change in your life is to search out the deep-seated beliefs that are blocking you from becoming more than you currently are. All self-change begins with changing your beliefs. Hypnosis and sleep programming programs are designed to create new beliefs or reprogram old beliefs.

Beliefs generate your thoughts and emotions, which in turn create your experiences. Your beliefs are the result of two things:

1. Present-life programming resulting from experiences and influences from factors such as parents, siblings, friends, church, and society.
2. Past-life experiences, which may have generated core beliefs that you retain in this lifetime. These can relate to your relationships or lack of relationships, career, success, and everything else in your existence.

You can't change what you don't recognize, so it's necessary to become aware of blocking beliefs. Here's a simple technique that will allow everyday experience to supply the awareness:

Your emotions are communicating a message. Every emotion is created by (and symbolizes) a belief. Take a moment to recall a fully experienced emotion. Now explore the belief behind the emotion, which will explain your reaction.

As an example, Alex got angry when his wife took too long getting ready to accompany him to a restaurant. His discomfort occurred because his wife did not do what he expected her to do, which in his mind amounted to a lack of love on her part. If we look a little deeper, it's easy to see Alex believes that his wife wants to control everything they do as a couple—an assumption that will eventually under-mine his marriage.

Your emotions are a form of energy that generates ever-changing states of feeling, which dovetail into each other. All negative emotions can be traced back to fearful beliefs. Dick often spent entire seminar days assisting participants to ferret out beliefs that keep them stuck at an unacceptable career level, to release old pain, or to throw off sexual hang-ups. But until you understand how beliefs work against you, you're not likely to spend much time exploring them.

To make a strong point, Dick would sometimes tell sem-inar or workshop participants to finish a sentence he would begin: "Don't even think about it; just instantly finish the sentence with the first words that jump into your mind," he would say. "OK, here's the first sentence: I think rich people are . . ."

After a few moments, he would ask the participants to tell him how they finished the sentence. Someone might say, "snobs." Another person might say, "lucky," or "unethi-cal," or "dishonest," or "thieves who stole the money."

In regard to these responses, we must understand a couple of human-potential concepts:

You cannot become what you resent.

You will always live up to your self-image.

If deep down you believe that if you become rich, you'll become dishonest, you'll never allow it to happen. It's that simple. If you believe that rich people are lucky, that doesn't help either: since you're not rich, you're not lucky. You cer-tainly couldn't accept a self-image of a snob, so again you avoid potential for wealth.

In one seminar, a participant said, "I think rich people are to be emulated."

"You're on your way to riches," Dick told him.

Once you're aware of your core beliefs, catch yourself every time you experience a negative belief. Reverse the programming by consciously expressing a contrasting positive belief. For most of us, it takes a bit of an effort, but it's well worth it.

Here's a concept to consider:

Everything that surrounds you is an extension of you. Your mate, children, home, furniture, car, pets, yard, office, and career are all physical expressions of your belief system and attitudes. Your environment is a manifestation of your energy and core beliefs, expressing your self-image and cultural overview.

And what mind has created, mind can change.

Change begins with the acceptance of new beliefs. Beliefs generate your thoughts and emotions, which create your experiences. If you aren't happy with your current life and want to change it, you need to change your core beliefs about allowing yourself to experience what you desire.

Your disharmonious beliefs are like a cage, restricting your potential and your life. If you want to escape from the cage, you must first recognize that it exists and you're not free.

You cannot change what you do not recognize.

Sadly, most people are unaware they exist in a self-created prison. What can you learn about yourself by examining your key life areas as an extension of you—as manifestations of your energy and core beliefs?

Your mate?

Your children?

Your home?

Your furniture?

Your car?

Your pets?

Your yard?

Your office?

Your career?

Let's say, for example, that your yard and office are a mess. This may be manifesting a lack of control in your life. You would be served by cleaning up these areas as first steps in taking control of your life. Explore how this lack of control is reflected in other areas.

If your primary relationship no longer reflects who you are, explore your part in creating the way it is. Who have you become? Then consider what you desire to happen. Be honest. Once you have clarity of intent, you can begin to program new beliefs in keeping with your desires.

Programming

Behavior wags the tail of feelings, so act in keeping with your desires and new feelings will follow. Visualize what you desire as if it were already so. Create vivid mental movies in which you're living the life you desire to live. Leave personalities out of the visualizations. If you visualize your mate doing something you want them to do, but it isn't in keeping with who they are, you're using negative energy and creating karma. Instead, visualize yourself living the life you desire with a loving mate—visualized facelessly. That way, if it's your karma to bond with someone new, you're not programming yourself into a corner.

Also, in meditation or self-hypnosis, give yourself positive suggestions worded as if what you desire were already accomplished. Self-talk—positive affirmations spoken out loud while you're driving or home alone—is also powerful programming.

Reinventing Yourself

Reinventing yourself is easy.

All you have to do is decide what you want and discover what is keeping you from having it. Then rise above the effects of the traps that are blocking you, and approach your goals in a realistic way. Easier said than done? Of course, but you can reinvent yourself if you are sincere in your quest and willing to proceed one step at a time.

To begin, if your life is not working the way you want it to work, you need to examine the nature of your traps. More often than not, there is no difference between yourself and the trap. This being the case, you are not trapped. Reinventing yourself begins by addressing what Dick regarded as the fifteen critical traps from a metaphysical/human-potential perspective.

Critical to reinventing yourself is the ability to choose wisely between realistic and unrealistic behavior—what we call *reason*. This relates to most of the critical traps. If you were to go into psychotherapy, the therapist would work to get you to be more responsible and realistic about your decisions, and to show you the value in making immediate sacrifices for the sake of long-term satisfaction.

Therapists usually work from the premise that you have problems because you are unable to fulfill your essential needs. We all have the same needs, but we differ in our ability to fulfill them. The severity of your symptoms is a direct reflection of your inability to fulfill those needs. But whatever your symptoms, they will disappear when your needs are aligned with reality and successfully fulfilled.

The practice of psychiatry is concerned with two basic psychological needs:

The need to love and be loved. You need at least one person in your life to love and who loves you in return. Without this essential person, you will be unable to fulfill your basic needs.

The need to feel worthwhile to yourself and others. To maintain high self-esteem, you must maintain a satisfactory standard of behavior and correct yourself when you are wrong. If your behavior is below your standard and you don't correct it, you will suffer as a result. You must fulfill your needs in a way that does not deprive others of the ability to fulfill their needs.

When you decide what behaviors are not serving you, be aware that an immediate change in behavior will lead to a change in attitude. You don't have to change how you feel about something to affect it—if you are willing to change what you are doing.

Exerting the self-discipline to make immediate changes in your behavior will lead to improved ways of meeting your needs and further improved behavior, which will increase your self-esteem.

What Dick called the Critical 15 was the foundation of reinventing yourself. We will explore these in the next chapter.

Introduction for New Hypnotism Students

Before stepping up to a seminar podium or sitting down for a one-to-one counseling session, remind yourself of the following:

Project warmth and power! Keep your mind like calm water.

Be with them totally! Get a sense of who they are by using these techniques:

1. Read their somatotype, clothing, attitude, educational level, etc.
2. Continually monitor their body language.
3. Use face reading.
4. Judge how they relate to the world: visually, auditorily, or kinesthetically.
5. Listen to the words between the words, and listen for key words.
6. Be psychic. Go for a one-word or one-line reading. (Examples: "Guilt-ridden," "Resisting wife's independence.")
7. Listen for the Critical 15 clues. (See sidebar.)
8. Establish rapport.

Answer with questions! Let them attain their own insights.

The Critical 15

With all emotional problems, the cause of the turmoil will always be one or more of these fifteen traps.

1. Beliefs
2. Assumed limitations and faulty assumptions
3. Blaming and victimhood
4. Negative payoffs
5. Masks or acts
6. Incompatible goals and values
7. Resistance to "what is"
8. Mirroring
9. Fear
10. The need to be right
11. Expectations
12. Lack of clarity
13. Lack of aliveness or motivation
14. Lack of self-discipline
15. Misplaced passion

Stress over and over that karma is the basis of reality. What is, is. This is difficult for many people to fully understand. Keep at it. Karma is or it isn't. There is no halfway. Either everything is karmic or nothing is karmic. Detached mind is a way to resolve suffering. This is total acceptance of what is, without resistance.

Establish clarity of intent. This will be a primary issue. Force participants/clients against the wall on this one: "If you don't know what you want, how do you ever expect to get it?

Nobody else can decide what you should want. It's up to you and you alone. If you don't decide, that's OK, but everything will stay exactly the way it is. What do you want?"

Accept self-responsibility. In accepting karma, you accept that you and you alone are responsible for your life just as it is. Play this from many angles.

Does who you are and what you do work for you? If so, make it all right with yourself. If not, use this awareness to create a new reality.

Create your own reality! You absolutely have the power and ability to create any reality you want to live if you're halfway realistic about what you desire.

Setting the Process into Motion

In a seminar training room: The trainer gives a short talk, then puts the participants into an altered state of consciousness and asks them questions which they answer subjectively. (Prior to awakening the group, the trainer often plays a song with powerful appropriate lyrics.) When the participants are awake, the trainer asks for verbal sharing in response to the altered-state process.

There are numerous ways to get participants to share. Examples:

- Make a statement and ask for their response.
- Get them to talk about their troubles in a particular life area.
- Put them in groups of two, three, or four, and have them interact. Afterwards, talk about what came up for them.

- In a one-on-one counseling session: Get your subject to talk about their problem (what they want). Get them to tell you what they want.

Establish rapport by mirroring body language. If they're upset, acknowledge their upset, but respond in a calm, placating voice tone. Use words that reflect the way they orient to the world (auditory, kinesthetic, or visual).

As they speak, listen for any of the Critical 15 clues, which will give you the opportunity to begin to ask questions. Never give them answers. Participant and subjects must come up with their own insights. In most sharing situations, you will probably hear more than one of the fifteen clues. Decide which is best to begin with. Then begin to ask questions that will eventually move you toward the action required. (See the previous chapter, "Reinventing Yourself.")

As you begin to ask the questions, you'll have to decide which of the seven basic techniques you will use to guide the participant/subject down a path to insight:

- Support. A gentle loving or spiritual approach.
- Shock. Verbally beat them up fast.
- Weave them into awareness.
- Attack or insult.
- Tease, toy; play cat and mouse with them.
- Appear to sympathize and agree. Then, when the time is right, pull the rug out from under them.
- Irritate them purposely to make them angry.

Tip: If you are attempting to get to the bottom of a major problem, hang-up, or phobia, and the participant/subject is showing no emotion, they are probably repressing their emotions. Keep them verbally "riding the sword." The moment they move off the issue, move them back, firmly. The more upset they get, the more likely you are to break through. Watch for pupils dilating, lips quivering, voice shaking, eyes beginning to water, and avoidance of eye contact. Use these signals to generate catharsis, if the individual is physically healthy enough to handle it, and if you are sure enough of your own ability to handle it.

At the point of catharsis, you have generated a brain phase and the participant/subject is open to new programming in the form of positive suggestions that override the old problem.

Tip: Explore your subject's beliefs and the consequences of their beliefs. Beliefs drive behavior, so what actions result from the beliefs? Behavior is belief in action. The bottom line: if you want to change your life, you must change your beliefs. Test beliefs against "what is."

Tip: If your subject becomes angry at you, you can probably turn their anger into catharsis. As an example, you might explore displacement: "Who else causes you to feel this kind of anger?" "You're holding back; what do you really want to say to me?" Give the anger a size, shape, color. Process. Go back to cause.

Tip: When the cause of the problem is unknown or to relive a situation that retains negative energy, use back-to-the-cause hypnotic regression. Know that if they become upset about a past incident in regression, the situation is still **affecting them and has never been** "completed." Get them to totally experience this past (causal) situation in regression. Get them to express their anger and repressed emotions. If they are experiencing repressed anger toward a particular individual, get them to speak up and say what they really want to say—to shout it with emotion. Once this is completed, before awakening, get them to forgive themselves and the others involved.

Tip: In working with your subject to alter their viewpoint, as homework, suggest G.I. Gurdjieff's detachment technique of refusing to identify with a negative emotion: "Well, obviously, John's getting upset because he isn't getting his way." "It looks like John is feeling insecure about this meeting." This distancing makes it easier to identify the fear-based emotions and detach from them.

Make sure your participant/subject knows how to use follow-up reprogramming techniques, audios, and other materials. Once they know the cause, get them to include the following phrase in their daily programming: *In knowing the cause, I release the effect and forgive myself and everyone else involved.*

Responses and Techniques

These are typical of those used in human-potential trainings such as Bushido, Erhard Seminars Training (est), Lifespring, and Insight Training.

Beliefs: Shoot down your participant's/subject's beliefs. Beliefs are things you do not know from your experience. You may think you know them, you may even be willing to stake your life on them, but that doesn't make them reality.

"Beliefs destroy experience!" (This is key to changing viewpoint.)

"Until you base your life on experience instead of beliefs, your life will never work as well as it can."

"Any reaction you have toward me is a belief."

"Belief in God kills God. By not having a belief in God, you can begin to experience God."

"Beliefs are B.S. = bullshit!"

When a participant/subject is unwilling to share the "real stuff" or is avoiding, you can use these tactics:

- This isn't going anywhere.
- You're stuffing it! When are you going to release?
- Stop stuffing it.
- Do you know silence is a cop-out?
- If I were you and you were me, what kind of a mask would you say I was wearing?
- Why do I feel like you're stuffing it when I talk to you?
- What is it about sharing that bothers you?
- Be straight! (If you keep repeating this, it is very powerful.)

When responding to an observation, an opinion, or a conclusion that you don't want to get verbally involved in, you can say:

- Those are your observations. I can't argue with you on them, because they are your observations (or opinions or conclusions).
- Thank you for sharing. (Then, in a seminar, recognize the next person to share with the group.)

Dialogue from *The Book of est*:

Participant: I don't understand.

Trainer: Don't try to understand. Understanding doesn't work—just experience.

Participant: You're a stupid fascist.

Trainer: That's not an experience, asshole, that's a belief. Look at your experience. I want you to get in touch with your feelings right now.

Participant: I'm mad.

Trainer: That's closer. Exactly what are you feeling right now?

Participant: My muscles are tense, and my stomach is churning, and you're a fascist.

Trainer: Good, two experiences and a belief.

More response and encounter techniques:

- If you feel a participant/subject isn't paying attention, or if the room energy appears to be dropping, pick a participant, point at them and say, "What did I just say?"

If they can't repeat it, say, "See, your subconscious mind is threatened by the communications. It is putting you to sleep. Stop avoiding. Be with me now!"

To build anxiety in the room, or within an individual participant, say, "You know what I think?" Then slowly walk across the room toward them while maintaining a stern expression.

If you want the participant/subject to continue a roll of finding their own answers, say, "All right, what is under that?" Or, "Good, now we're making some headway. Now what's behind that?"

If you want time to scratch your ass, if you feel intimidated, insecure, or just want a moment to yourself, yell, "Freeze! Close your eyes and think about this issue for a few moments."

If you're being attacked: "What do you think you'd be thinking if I'd said that to you?"

Don't let the participant/subject lead you off purpose. MAINTAIN CONTROL! "Riding the Sword" is the technique of keeping them on the point.

In a seminar: If, out of nervousness or to seek your approval, the group applauds and it is not appropriate, say, "I'm not here for your applause or approval."

In a seminar: When a participant is withholding, is especially callous, or just doesn't get it, you can use the group against them, by asking for a show of hands:

"How many think she is avoiding?" (Raise your hand, so they will follow.) "How many think she is being honest?"

Then "OK, that's what your Universe is hearing. I want you to sit down and think about it."

Variations:

"These people all know your act."

"How many of you can see yourself in her?"

In a seminar: Watch for anyone closing their eyes, which is usually an "avoid." Yell, "Keep your eyes open back there!" This is good to do every so often even if no one is closing their eyes. It increases attention, for they feel you are sweeping the room visually, watching for such things.

Continually stress win-win situations. If one wins and the other loses, both lose.

If an individual or a significant percentage of the group is demonstrating closed body language, call them on it: "Stop closing down! When you display open body language, you're open to new ideas. So stop crossing your legs and arms."

If someone thinks they are altruistic, make sure they understand that everyone operates in their own self-interest all the time.

In a seminar: After a one-on-one cathartic tearjerker, turn to the group and ask, "What was going on with you as you listened to her story?" (This can be a quickie group meditation, or a longer altered-state process, or you can call upon one individual.)

Some may object that when you settle one problem, there is always something new you have to deal with. Reply with: "You never get life totally handled. You tear down a cage and find that there is another cage beyond it, but the next one is a little larger."

After an especially sad story that has changed the energy in the room, somehow get the participant to light-heartedly step out of the situation and look back upon it. (Examples: "Why do you suppose you karmically experience that?" "All our important experiences are karmic and designed to teach us something. What did you learn as a result of this?" "No matter how terrible, every experience bears a gift. What was the gift in this for you?")

As a trainer/counselor, you must not show pity:

"I don't pity you, because if I do, I'm just supporting your negative energy."

When a participant/subject claims, "I don't know what to do," say, "OK, that's fine. That's a fine game to play. You know exactly what to do. You know what the answer is. Either you're willing to talk about it now, or you're not willing to talk about it now. I'm not going to buy into your fog. If you want to pretend you don't know what's going on, I don't want to play." (In a seminar, motion for the participant to sit down and walk away. In a one-on-one session, go quiet and see what the client says in response.)

You can also use the following story to distinguish between pity and compassion: You come upon a drowning man, but you don't know how to swim. Sympathy: you jump in the river and drown with him. This is a pity party. Empathy: you sit down and moan and cry about his drowning. Compassion: You do something about it. Throw him a rope, or run and find someone who knows how to swim.

When a participant is looking for you to provide the answer, say:

"It's your life. If that happened to me in my life, I have certain things I would do, being the person I am. But it would be foolish for you to try to live my life. My answers don't fit you. What do you want? What do you want to do? What are the prices, and what are the rewards involved in the choices you have?"

More responses, including ones to use when you don't have a response:

"I don't have the faintest idea how to respond to that."

"Who do you think you're kidding?"

"Do you want to explore that?"

"Anyone else in the room want to get involved in that?"

"What is it you're really saying? I feel attacked by you."

"You could not conceive of the question unless you already knew the answer. So you tell me what you should do."

"The Universe can only give you what you're willing to accept."

"I've got a lot of answers, but they're of no value for you. This is for you to find your own answers."

"I will answer clarification questions, but I will answer most of your questions with a question because I want you to come up with your own answers."

When a participant/subject wants to argue: "There aren't going to be any debates in here. Debates turn into arguments, and there is no point to it."

If they ask a question you can't answer: "Good question. This is your session; you're the one who has the answers."

If you feel stressed, say, "*Stop*. Close your eyes and go deep within. Do this all on your own while I am quiet for a few moments." Or give the participant/client something to meditate about.

If you feel stressed in a seminar, simply stop what you are doing and stare at the group with a serious look on your face for about five seconds. Then ask a question. The dramatic pause is extremely powerful.

In response to someone attacking you: "I am whatever you think I am. There is a lot of wisdom in that statement if you're astute enough to perceive it."

"What is it about that that bothers you?"

Regression Scale

All divisions of hypnotic depth are arbitrary. One scoring system uses 50 divisions, another 30, another 21, and there are several which divide the stages in from 3 to 9 categories. In communicating to the public, I talk about three: light, medium, and deep hypnosis. Professionally Dick used six divisions as they relate to regressive hypnosis.

Stage 1: Hypnoidal/lethargic stage. The subject feels relaxed but is aware of activities in the room. His fingers may feel a bit tingly, but there is no real feeling of trance. Fantasy regression impressions. Subject feels he is making it up, and he may be.

Stage 2: Light sleep. The subject is more relaxed, but the conscious mind is still active. He feels he could open his eyes if he wanted, but he won't try. His body probably feels heavy, and he could feel a floating or swaying sensation. Fantasy regression impressions as an observer, usually without emotion.

Stage 3: Medium sleep. The subject is still aware of activities in the room, but will pay no attention. He would respond to eye and arm catalepsy in tests. Fantasy regression impressions, but the fantasy seems to take over on its own. When he allows his conscious mind to become involved, he has to "reset" the fantasy. Some emotion possible during regression.

Stage 4: Medium/deep sleep. The subject no longer needs to begin the impressions via fantasy. He will feel the emotions in a situation, but still seems to be an observer more often than a participant or "re-liver" at this stage. You may or may not be able to block memories of his experiences. If you ask him to open his eyes, desiring that he remain in a trance, he may actually awaken.

Stage 5: Somnambulism. The subject can open his eyes without coming out of trance. Smell and taste hallucinations can be created. Posthypnotic suggestions will be fulfilled. The subject will "relive" the past life unless commanded to become an observer. He often sees through his own eyes and will sometimes question where you are because he can't see you.

Stage 6: Deep somnambulism/plenary. The subject is totally unaware of physical surroundings and will completely "relive" his past. All types of hypnotic phenomena are possible. He is capable of a form of mental projection, as opposed to astral projection, into the past or present.

Important Considerations You Should Be Aware Of

In a seminar, before using a strobe light, brain wave synchronizer, or any pulsating light, be sure to ask if any epileptics are present. This light effect can be conducive to convulsions. Epileptics should simply cover their eyes.

The subject who won't wake up. Never panic, or allow anyone else present to panic, for there is absolutely nothing to worry about.

1. Be firm but kind, and demand that the subject wake up on the count of five. Then count up.
2. Raise an eyelid and blow short, sharp breaths directly on the eye.
3. If all else fails, simply let them sleep it off. They will awaken within a few hours at most.
4. (For private clients only.) Let them know you will charge them every minute they sleep, beginning now. (Come up with a large rate.)

Refractory subjects. Don't give up on subjects who seem impossible to hypnotize. I have yet to find a subject that is not capable of at least a light trance.

If you're dealing with a subject that you feel might become extremely upset, give them the advance suggestion: "If I touch you on the arm and say the words, 'Let go,' you will immediately let go of the past-life impressions and return to the present, feeling totally calm and relaxed. You will immediately respond to my command of 'let go' and all mental impressions will fade away, instantly! This is an absolute command you will carry out." I usually give this suggestion to all participants when conducting a stage demonstration.

Male practitioners should have a third party present or ask if they can film the session when hypnotizing female subjects, especially if there seems to be any possibility that the subject is disturbed.

Hysterical cases of extreme laughing or crying can scare spectators and cause them to lose confidence in you. No harm is going to come to the subject, but for obvious reasons such scenes are to be avoided. Watch for initial signs: a rhythmic back-and-forth movement of the head. The person could begin to rock or sway in a circular motion. Exaggerated breathing also often accompanies this effect. This means that the subject is beginning to become hysterical; you should stop the induction and begin to calm your subject. In a private session, you can make a judgment about whether to continue or not. In public, I would slowly bring the subject back to consciousness. If an hysterical episode actually gets started, under no condition should you immediately awaken the subject, but instead make many calming suggestions, and allow the hysteria to dissipate. This could take a good half hour.

Learn to monitor your subjects' muscle relaxation. Watch the veins in the neck for an accelerating pulse rate, or feel their pulse by holding their wrist. The average pulse is 76.

When testing subjects, beware of rapid cooperation on the part of the subject. Real responses are slow and often jerky. In a balloon and book test, if the arm instantly shoots up in the air, the subject is probably faking. (The balloon and book test: to test how deep our subject is in hypnosis, you can tell them to hold out both hands while you place a "book" in their right hand, and tie a "balloon" in their left hand.)

If you become involved with much regressive hypnosis, it is very likely that you'll have subjects that find themselves in the "lower astral plane" on the other side. This experience is usually described as dark, damp, and fearful. The subject can only see shadowlike forms and is highly confused. Be aware that they are in a state between a lifetime of low awareness and rebirth. Gently guide them forward into the next incarnation.

Channel contact. Always be on the lookout for a patterned channel voice. On occasion it seems that a discarnate entity, or another aspect of the subject's own personality, is capable of using the vocal cords to communicate. If you desire to let this happen, be firm and allow no negativity to begin. At the first sign of any hissing, swearing, or similar form of communication, begin immediate exorcism procedures. This could be the ultimate test of your ability to maintain your cool, should it ever happen. It doesn't matter if this is real or the manifestation of a belief system. The results and the way of handling it will be the same.

Be totally calm and intensify your firmness and command of the situation. If the entity threatens you, respond like this: "Since you are aware enough to be here, you are certainly aware enough to know that I have a hundred times your power. I can call upon aid from the higher realms, and I can manifest intense energy and powers of my own. If you continue to be a problem, I shall be forced to have you taken care of in a way you will find most unpleasant . . . and you know I can do it. Now I am going to count from five to one, and on the count of one, you shall be gone, and John Jones will again take control of his own vocal chords. I am now giving John my own energy, which I feed to him through my hands [for public demonstrations], and I ask that others in the room come up and lay their hands upon John and give him even more energy. [For private sessions, call in the Archangels or other God entities you work with]. And we are now intensifying the white light protection . . . number five . . . and you are now leaving . . ." Continue to chatter firmly as you count backward, then, on the count of one, in a loud, firm voice, pronounce that the entity is gone, never to return again.

You can talk to the entity and try to find out about its confusion. If it doesn't realize it is dead, explain that. Have it look around until it sees a spot of light, then go to it. There are many other techniques. I talk about some in my book *You Were Born to Be Together*. *Thirty Years Among the Dead*, by Dr. Carl Wickland and Rev. Steven Earl York, is probably the best book available on this subject.

Thought Language

Using thought language in meditation and hypnosis is a matter of silently, subjectively sending out a thought, then listening for an internal answer, which may be perceived as another thought, a feeling, or a fantasy-like visualization. Don't expect a voice to literally speak in your ear; instead, be alert for gentle intuitive feelings, ideas, and awareness. These may very well be directed from your own Guides, Masters, or those whom you sent to contact. You'll soon sense when you are in contact, and with a little practice, you'll be able to judge the validity of your experience.

Thought language is the primary way to receive information during meditation and hypnosis and to communicate with your Guides, loved ones, and Masters.

The air around you is filled with radio and TV messages, but you can't hear them until your receiver is turned on and tuned to the station you want to hear. The air around you is also filled with voices of spirits, which you can't hear until you open to receive them.

You hold the power to decide what messages you will receive and the spiritual level you will be attuned to.

If you use protective invocations, if you have a high level of awareness, and if you sincerely desire to contact only highly evolved and loving entities, then mischievous or negative spirits cannot get through. Highly evolved souls won't command you; instead they will gently guide you toward expanded awareness.

The more you develop this technique, the more effective it will become. Always be aware that you're in control in a hypnosis or meditation session. If you feel uncomfortable in any way, just awaken yourself by counting up from one to five and telling yourself you're wide awake.

Part Two
SCRIPTS FOR HYPNOSIS SESSIONS

Countdown and Awaken

These are the two basic scripts for inducing a hypnotic trance and awakening a client from a trance. They are incorporated into most of the scripts in part 2, but here they are on their own.

Countdown

As you focus upon the sound of my voice, I am going to count you down, down, down . . . so vividly imagine yourself in a situation going down . . . walking down stairs, downhill, down the side of a pyramid . . . or any situation in which you see yourself going down, while I count backwards from seven to one.

Number seven, deeper, deeper, deeper, down, down, down. Number six, deeper, deeper, deeper, down, down, down.

Number five, deeper, deeper, deeper, down, down, down.

Number four, deeper, deeper, deeper, down, down, down.

Number three, deeper, deeper, deeper, down, down, down.

Number two, deeper, deeper, deeper, down, down, down.

Number one, deeper, deeper, deeper, down, down, down.

And you're relaxed and at ease, and you feel deep. But let's go down a little deeper now . . . deeper now.

Number seven, deeper, deeper, deeper, down, down, down. Number six, deeper, deeper, deeper, down, down, down.

Number five, deeper, deeper, deeper, down, down, down.

Number four, deeper, deeper, deeper, down, down, down.

Number three, deeper, deeper, deeper, down, down, down.

Number two, deeper, deeper, deeper, down, down, down.

Number one, deeper, deeper, deeper, down, down, down.

And you are now completely relaxed and at ease. And if you feel uncomfortable at any time, you can easily bring yourself up by counting up from one to five and say the words, "Wide awake."

Awaken

And in just a moment I'm going to wake you up. On the count of five, you will open your eyes and be wide awake, fully alert, thinking, and acting with calm self-assurance. You'll awaken feeling as if you've just taken a relaxing nap, and you'll be at peace with yourself, the world, and every-one in it.

Number one, coming on up now and feeling an expanding spiritual light within.

Number two, coming up feeling at peace with all life.

Number three, coming on up and tapping into an internal balance and harmony.

Number four, recall the situation in the room.

And number five, wide awake, wide awake. Open your eyes and feel good. Number five, wide awake.

Abundance Body Relaxation

You're breathing deeply and relaxing completely. Breathing deeply and relaxing completely . . . and allowing a quietness of spirit to come in. Taking a deep breath in and holding it as long as you comfortably can . . . then let the breath out slowly through slightly parted lips, and when the breath is all the way out, push it further out, and further out . . . and then repeat the process. Breathing deeply, and when any outside thoughts come into your mind, simply brush them aside and tell yourself, "I'll deal with that later," and then return your concentration to the sound of my voice, and breathing deeply and relaxing completely.

And in just a moment I'm going to relax your body one part at a time. So play the role, play the part, and feel your body relaxing as I ask you to do so. And the relaxing power is coming into the toes of both of your feet at the same time . . . and it's moving right on down into the balls of your feet, into your arches, into your heels, and right on up to your ankles.

Completely relaxed, completely relaxed . . . and the relaxing sensations now move on up your legs to your knees, relaxing all the muscles as it goes. And on up your legs now, to your thighs and to your hips. Permeating every cell and every atom.

And you're relaxing completely, relaxing completely, keeping your full attention on the sound of my voice and relaxing your body, as the relaxing sensations move on down into the fingers of both of your hands . . . relaxing your hands. Feel your hands relaxing. And your lower arms are relaxed, and your upper arms are relaxed. Fingers and hands and lower arms and upper arms . . . just completely relaxed.

And the relaxing sensations now move on down into the base of your spine, your root chakra. Imagine a warmth in your root chakra as if a ray of sunlight were coming into the room and falling upon your spine . . . and it feels good. You imagine this warmth now moving up your spine . . . up your spine . . . up your spine and into the back of your neck and shoulder muscles. And your shoulder muscles are now loose and limp . . . loose and limp . . . just completely relaxed. And the relaxing sensations now move on up the back of your neck and into your scalp. Relaxing your scalp. Feel your scalp relaxing and feel the relaxing sensations now drain down into your facial muscles, relaxing your facial muscles. Your jaw is relaxed. Allow a little space between your teeth. And your throat is relaxed.

Your entire body is now relaxed all over in every way. And all tension is gone from your body and mind.

And we're now going to balance and energize your aura and attune you to the subtle vibrations that support the perception of subjective awareness. So to begin, imagine a beam of iridescent white light coming down from above and entering your crown chakra of spirituality on the top

of your head. Imagine the light . . . create it with the unlimited power of your mind. This is the Universal light of life energy, and you feel it stimulating this chakra center, which is purple in color. Visualize a swirling vortex of purple and the light opens, balances, and charges this chakra center. Imagine the opening, balancing, charging.

(Pause for five seconds.)

And the light is now moving on down into the center of your forehead—your brow chakra, which is a swirling blue-violet vortex of energy. Perceive the blue-violet color, and feel the balancing and energizing that is taking place here. Opening, balancing, energizing.

(Pause for five seconds.)

And the light is now moving on down into your throat chakra, which is a swirling silvery-blue vortex of energy. Perceive the silvery-blue color, and feel the balancing and energizing that is taking place here. Opening, balancing, energizing.

(Pause for five seconds.)

And the light is now moving on down into your heart chakra, which is to be perceived as a golden glow. Perceive the golden color, and feel the balancing and energizing of your heart chakra center. Opening, balancing, energizing.

(Pause for five seconds.)

And the light is now moving on down into your solar plexus chakra, located at the level of your navel. This chakra is to be visualized as several shades of red in color. Perceive the red colors, and imagine the balancing and energizing that is taking place here. Opening, balancing, energizing.

(Pause for five seconds.)

And the light is moving on down into your sacral or spleen chakra, which is located a little below your navel. This swirling vortex of energy is a rainbow of colors. Perceive the many colors, and feel the balancing and energizing that is taking place here. Opening, balancing, energizing.

(Pause for five seconds.)

And the light is now moving on down into your root chakra at the base of your spine. This chakra is to be visualized as a swirling vortex of energy, red and orange in color. Perceive the reds and oranges, and feel the balancing and energizing that is taking place here. Opening, balancing, energizing.

(Pause for five seconds.)

And your chakras are opened, balanced, and charged, thus expanding your aura and attuning you to the subtle vibrations that support the perception of subjective awareness.

And it's now time to imagine the bright white light moving back up into heart area.

Visualize your heart center overflowing with the Universal light of life energy.

And now imagine the light emerging from your heart center to surround your body in a protective aura of bright white God light.

And you are totally protected. Totally protected. Only your own Guides and Masters or highly evolved and loving entities who mean you well will be able to influence you in any way in this altered state of consciousness session.

And as you continue to focus upon the sound of my voice, I am going to count you down, down, down . . . so vividly imagine yourself in a situation going down . . . walking down stairs, downhill, down the side of a pyramid . . . or any situation in which you see yourself going down, while I count backwards from seven to one.

Number seven, deeper, deeper, deeper, down, down, down. Number six, deeper, deeper, deeper, down, down, down.

Number five, deeper, deeper, deeper, down, down, down.

Number four, deeper, deeper, deeper, down, down, down.

Number three, deeper, deeper, deeper, down, down, down.

Number two, deeper, deeper, deeper, down, down, down.

Number one, deeper, deeper, deeper, down, down, down.

And you're relaxed and at ease, and you feel deep. But let's go down a little deeper now . . . deeper now.

Number seven, deeper, deeper, deeper, down, down, down. Number six, deeper, deeper, deeper, down, down, down.

Number five, deeper, deeper, deeper, down, down, down.

Number four, deeper, deeper, deeper, down, down, down.

Number three, deeper, deeper, deeper, down, down, down.

Number two, deeper, deeper, deeper, down, down, down.

Number one, deeper, deeper, deeper, down, down, down.

And a quietness of spirit permeates your body and mind . . . and you can awaken on your own at any time by counting up from one to five and saying the words, "Wide awake." So you're in control, and you can awaken at any time.

But now take a few moments to send loving thoughts to your God within . . . who is always there within you, ready to cocreate with you. There is only one power in the Universe, and we call it God. Mystic Neville Goddard says, "God is a person because you are a person. He becomes you, as He becomes us all, that we may become who He is." So imagine that God inside of you. There is nothing outside of you until you create an external world with the power of your mind—by imagining a world you desire.

Think about this: there is nothing outside of yourself, but working with your God inside of you, together, you can act to mentally create an external world by imagining a reality based upon your visualizations and feelings.

Vividly imagine communing with your God within. Get to know each other, and consider how your request for abundance can serve your greater good, the greater good of your family, the country, and the greater good of all mankind.

(Pause for sixty seconds.)

You are worthy and deserving of the very best life has to offer. I am now going to share some words of abundance . . .

"I project power and confidence at all times. I know exactly what I want, and I get it. I am enthusiastic and willing to act. I am persistent, ambitious, and determined. I now manifest abundance. I now make large amounts of money. I create great wealth. My creative thinking now opens the door to great monetary abundance. Whatever I can imagine I can create. And so it is."

And now it is time to repeat this request for abundance. Say the words along with me: "I project power and confidence at all times. I know exactly what I want, and I get it. I am persistent, ambitious, and determined. I now make money. I make large amounts of money. I create great wealth. My creative thinking now opens the door to great monetary abundance. Whatever I can imagine I can create. And so it is."

And it's now time to imagine and *feel* what it will feel like to get what you want. Share this with God, who assists you in this manifestation. The secret is to sense how good it *feels* to project power and confidence . . . and to be persistent, ambitious, and determined at all times. And above all else, to create great abundance and to know your creative thinking now opens the door to great monetary abundance. Imagine and *feel*. How exciting it is to create life-changing concepts in your mind and manifest them in your conscious awareness. Feel this, feel your skin tingling with excitement. Sense the joy in your heart, and imagine the ripples of good spreading out and into your world . . . spreading the God light into the shadows, illuminating all who come in contact with you.

And I am going to be quiet for a couple of minutes while you imagine receiving exactly what you asked for. Vividly imagine it. Make it real. *Feel* how good it *feels* to have manifested what you desire.

(Pause for two and a half minutes.)

AND YOU HAVE JUST SEEN YOUR OWN REALITY! And from this moment on, you accept without questioning the reality of your forthcoming manifestation. Always visualize and feel your wish having manifested just before you fall asleep. When you awaken, open your eyes and awaken confident of your forthcoming manifestation success.

And it's now you can choose to awaken remembering everything that transpired in this session or to go to sleep. To awaken, count yourself up from one to five and say the words, "Wide awake."

To go to sleep, focus on the soft music, and drift off into a peaceful, relaxing sleep . . . a peaceful relaxing sleep . . . peaceful relaxing sleep . . . relaxing sleep . . . relaxing sleep . . . relaxing sleep . . .

Aliveness and Challenge

Dick would frequently precede this process with the following talk:

Aliveness is real enjoyment in doing what you do. It is the excitement and exhilaration that makes you glad to be alive. It is the joy, stimulation, and pleasure that makes life worth living.

But for most people, life is long on misery, short on joy, and short on aliveness.

Why? Because we have forgotten who and what we really are, and allow ourselves to get caught up in the game of life. We compromise and give away our freedom.

Society molds "ladies and gentlemen," which, to me, is another way of saying phonies and hypocrites. People who wear masks and proper attire. They adhere to proper manners and proper etiquette. Ladies and gentlemen do the "right" thing. They are conventional characters in a play. They are often so concerned with what other people think that they lose their own identity. When you accept the expectations of others, they can dominate, cripple and paralyze you. Expectations are enemies of freedom.

Dr. David Viscott says, "It takes free partners to make a relationship whole." In any relationship, the partners need to be free to do what they want to do. "When you allow your partner to be free, you also free yourself from being his keeper."

When you give away your freedom, you succumb to your fears. And you close down and burn out. Somewhere, usually from about age thirty-five on, people tend to burn out and just run on momentum. It's like riding a bike. It takes you a while to pump up to speed, but from that point on, you can keep the momentum going without a lot of effort.

But when you just run on momentum, your life gets boring. Maybe your career was once enjoyable, but sooner or later, to make your payments and fulfill your obligations, life and career become work. When life becomes routine, dull, boring, or mundane, many people seek places to hide. They seek aliveness in watching TV or "cosmic foo-foo" metaphysics. Or they drink, do drugs, or talk endlessly on the phone.

But your mind cannot take "boring" for long. If you don't make life interesting, your mind will create some excitement. Maybe you'll begin to fight with your mate. (When you're experiencing emotional pain, at least you know you're alive.) Or maybe you get sick or have an accident. Both will give you something to strive for.

When I was writing *You Were Born Again to Be Together*, I interviewed a physicist who worked in the atomic testing labs at White Sands, New Mexico. He told me he had been an atheist, but his work had him rethinking his beliefs. He said they were isolating the smallest molecule of energy in a sealed cloud chamber. Nothing else could get in; nothing could get out.

The molecule was smaller than an atom, so it could only be seen when photographed with ultra-high-sensitivity film. When they viewed the film, the molecule was living its life in the cloud chamber. It had size, weight, pattern, and speed. In time it slowed down and eventually fell to the bottom of the cloud chamber, appearing to die. But soon it was back, only now it had a new size, a new weight, a new pattern, and a new speed. The physicist said, "Energy cannot die; it can only transform. And I know I'm energy, so that means I cannot die. Maybe transformation is reincarnation."

You are energy, and energy cannot stand still. It will move forward expanding or backward, preparing to transform.

Do you know what makes energy move forward?

Aliveness and challenge.

This is important: As a natural expression of energy, that which is totally successful tends to destroy itself. If you allow yourself to attain total success in your relationship, your career, your spiritual awareness, you'll destroy it. You know this subconsciously. Once the lessons are learned, you will move on. So there is no way you should dare allow yourself to obtain total success in any area of your life.

The Universe functions as a yin/yang balance, resulting in tension between opposites. Yin = negative. Yang = positive. We all contain dual aspects: love/hate; harmony/chaos; good/evil. That which succeeds in becoming all yin or all yang tends to destroy itself. Examples:

- A couple struggles through years of adversity, but breaks up when life becomes easy.

- Historically, any country that has reached its peak has fragmented and collapsed when it was unopposed.
- Honest men who become extremely successful often become corrupt.
- The spiritual seeker who has attained awareness often manifests a crisis that starts his spiritual journey all over again.

Intuitively, you know you must express the yin/yang duality, because tension is necessary for structure to exist. And human beings are structure. Energy.

Don't think of positive and negative as good and bad. In this context, relate positive and negative to the plates in an automobile battery. One plate is charged positively, the next negatively, the next positively, and so on. The power to start your car is generated by the energy bouncing back and forth. The negative plate is not bad, and the positive plate is not good. They are simply what is.

Without tension, you don't exist. Thus there is a yin balance in your life. You can express it many ways, such as self-denial, excessive hard work, gambling, dangerous activities (such as driving too fast), arguing and fighting, and illness. War is the ultimate expression of yin energy.

The big question is: how can you allow yourself to be totally successful in your relationship, career, spirituality without destroying it?

The answer is *challenge*.

Back to what I first said about energy: unless you challenge yourself, your energy will stagnate and move backwards, preparing to transform by destroying itself.

So replace negative tension with positive challenge.

A young couple has struggled through adversity only to break up when life got easy—when there was no more challenge. Had they come up with their own positive challenge, there would have been no need to part.

The same is true with nations, which fragment and collapse when unopposed. At that point, the nation needs a positive new challenge. Instead of waging war, why not find a way to feed everyone and provide health services to all in need? That would be a challenge.

The secret here is to consciously direct challenge in a way that minimizes jeopardy while fulfilling the yin/yang balance. This is usually accomplished by *wise risking*.

Here's where it gets touchy. If you let challenge go too far, it will result in self-destruction. If you don't incorporate challenge into your life, that too will result in self-destruction. As an example of too much challenge, let's say you've learned to sail a boat, so you decide to sail to Hawaii. This is a challenge. But you haven't learned navigation, so you miss Hawaii and end up at the South Pole.

You must keep challenge in balance to obtain and maintain success. *So maybe it's time for you to start living more dangerously.*

Aliveness and Challenge Process

Let's do an altered state of consciousness process.

Much of the following process will amount to your coming up with either yes or no answers, but when I ask you a question in which you are exploring potentials, note the first thoughts that come into your mind in response to each question.

You're breathing deeply and relaxing completely.

Breathing deeply and relaxing completely . . . and allowing a quietness of spirit to come in. Taking a deep breath in and holding it as long as you comfortably can . . . then let the breath out slowly through slightly parted lips, and when the breath is all the way out, push it further out, and further out . . . and then repeat the process. Breathing deeply, and when any outside thoughts come into your mind, simply brush them aside and tell yourself, "I'll deal with that later." Then return your concentration to the sound of my voice, and breathing deeply and relaxing completely.

In just a moment I'm going to relax your body one part at a time. So play the role, play the part, and feel your body relaxing as I ask you to do so. And the relaxing power is coming into the toes of both of your feet at the same time . . . and it's moving right on down into the balls of your feet, into your arches, into your heels, and right on up to your ankles. Completely relaxed, completely relaxed . . . and the relaxing sensations now move on up your legs to your knees, relaxing all the muscles as it goes. And on up your legs now, to your thighs and to your hips. Permeating every cell and every atom.

And you're relaxing completely, relaxing completely, keeping your full attention on the sound of my voice and relaxing your body, as the relaxing sensations move on down into the fingers of both of your hands . . . relaxing your hands. Feel your hands relaxing. And your lower arms are relaxed, and your upper arms are relaxed. Fingers and hands and lower arms and upper arms . . . just completely relaxed.

And the relaxing sensations now move on down into the base of your spine, your root chakra. Imagine a warmth in your root chakra as if a ray of sunlight were coming into the room and falling upon your spine . . . and it feels good. You imagine this warmth now moving up your spine . . . up your spine . . . up your spine and into the back of your neck and shoulder muscles. And your shoulder muscles are now loose and limp . . . loose and limp . . . just completely relaxed. And the relaxing sensations now move on up the back of your neck and into your scalp. Relaxing your scalp. Feel your scalp relaxing, and feel the relaxing sensations now drain down into your facial muscles, relaxing your facial muscles. Your jaw is relaxed. Allow a little space between your teeth. And your throat is relaxed. Your entire body is now relaxed all over in every way. And all tension is gone from your body and mind.

And as you continue to focus upon the sound of my voice, I am going to count you down, down, down . . . so vividly imagine yourself in a situation going down . . . walking down stairs, downhill, down the side of a pyramid . . . or any situation in which you see yourself going down, while I count backwards from seven to one.

Number seven, deeper, deeper, deeper, down, down, down.

Number six, deeper, deeper, deeper, down, down, down. Number five, deeper, deeper, deeper, down, down, down. Number four, deeper, deeper, deeper, down, down, down. Number three, deeper, deeper, deeper, down, down, down.

Number two, deeper, deeper, deeper, down, down, down. Number one, deeper, deeper, deeper, down, down, down.

And you're relaxed and at ease, and you feel deep. But let's go down a little deeper now . . . deeper now.

Number seven, deeper, deeper, deeper, down, down, down.

Number six, deeper, deeper, deeper, down, down, down. Number five, deeper, deeper, deeper, down, down, down. Number four, deeper, deeper, deeper, down, down, down. Number three, deeper, deeper, deeper, down, down, down.

Number two, deeper, deeper, deeper, down, down, down. Number one, deeper, deeper, deeper, down, down, down.

And you're now relaxed and at ease, and you feel in balance and in harmony. A quietness of spirit permeates your body and mind.

All right, you're relaxed and at ease and ready to objectively explore your present levels of aliveness.

Aliveness is excitement . . . enjoyment in experiencing what you're experiencing. It's that blood-pumping exhilaration that makes you feel glad to be alive. The challenge and joy and stimulation and pleasure that make life worth living.

In this session, I'm going to be asking you many yes and no questions, and you'll judge the results . . . so first, let's look at your career, or if you don't have a career, explore the primary way you spend your time.

Do you presently experience aliveness in your career, yes or no?

(Pause for five seconds.)

Is there any real challenge in your career, yes or no?

(Pause for five seconds.)

Are you growing in your career, yes or no?

(Pause for five seconds.)

Are you satisfied with your career, yes or no?

(Pause for five seconds.)

OK . . . if you answered no to many of the questions, you are not living up to your career potential or you're stagnating.

If there is no real challenge in your career, what can you do to create challenge and aliveness? Would you have to start a new career, or alter your career, or change locations, or maybe do something on the side? The question is, "What can you do to create challenge and aliveness in your career or the primary way you spend your time?"

(Pause for sixty seconds.)

And now let's explore relationships. (I'll be phrasing each question two ways: one for those in a primary relationship and one for those desiring to establish a primary relationship.)

Do you presently experience aliveness in your primary relationship, yes or no?

(Pause for five seconds.)

If you are seeking a primary relationship, do you experience aliveness in your quest, yes or no?

(Pause for five seconds.)

Is there still challenge in your primary relationship, yes or no?

(Pause for five seconds.)

If you are seeking a primary relationship, do you experience challenge in the process, yes or no?

(Pause for five seconds.)

If you're in a primary relationship, are the two of you involved in stimulating activities that you share, other than sex, yes or no?

(Pause for five seconds.)

Are you growing in your relationship or as a result of seeking a relationship, yes or no?

(Pause for five seconds.)

Are you satisfied with the relationship side of your life, yes or no? (Pause for five seconds.)

Do you really communicate in your relationship, or with those you meet as you seek to establish a relationship, yes or no?

(Pause for five seconds.)

All right, again, if you answered no to many of these questions, you're stagnating or not living up to your potential for a warm, fulfilling relationship in which you share mutual personal growth.

So if there isn't enough aliveness and challenge in your relationship or your quest for one, what can you do to create aliveness and challenge?

(Pause for sixty seconds.)

All right, now let's explore your sex life. Do you presently experience aliveness in your sex life, yes or no?

(Pause for five seconds.)

Is there any real challenge in your sex life, yes or no?

(Pause for five seconds.)

Are you repressing your sexual desires in any way, yes or no?

(Pause for five seconds.)

Do you truly communicate your sexual desires to your partner, yes or no?

(Pause for five seconds.)

Are you satisfied with your sex life, yes or no?

(Pause for five seconds.)

Again, if you answered no to many of these questions, you're repressing or dissipating your sexual energy, so the question is, "What can you do to create aliveness in your sex life?"

Before you answer that question in your mind, be aware that sexual conduct should never cause pain to others or turbulence in ourselves. With that awareness in mind, what could you do to create aliveness in your sex life?

(Pause for sixty seconds.)

All right, the next questions are regarding your social life and social involvements.

First, do you presently experience aliveness in your social involvements, yes or no?

(Pause for five seconds.)

Is there still a challenge in your social life, yes or no?

(Pause for five seconds.)

Are you open to exploring new social avenues or fulfillment, yes or no?

(Pause for five seconds.)

Are you satisfied with your social life, yes or no?

(Pause for five seconds.)

OK . . . again, if you answered no to many of the questions, you are not living up to your potential for an exciting, challenging social life. So if there is no real aliveness in your social life, what can you do to create it?

(Pause for sixty seconds.)

And now the next questions are in regard to your spiritual searching. First, do you experience aliveness in your spiritual involvements and seeking, yes or no?

(Pause for five seconds.)

Is there still a challenge in your spiritual search, yes or no?

(Pause for five seconds.)

Are you still open to exploring new spiritual potentials, concepts and ideas, yes or no?

(Pause for five seconds.)

Are you really growing spiritually, yes or no?

(Pause for five seconds.)

If you answered no to many of these questions, you're probably spiritually stagnating, and the question is, "What can you do to generate aliveness in your spiritual life?"

(Pause for sixty seconds.)

All right, here's an important question. In what area of your life do you find the most aliveness and challenge?

(Pause for sixty seconds.)

This process is a good indicator of how much challenge you're experiencing in your life. Remember, stagnation is self-destruction, because energy can't stand still. It must move forward or backward—and you are energy.

So how about it? Are you experiencing aliveness, or is it time to consider living dangerously and creating some new challenges in your life? Is it? Maybe it's time to reject the dictates of society and the opinions of others and stop worrying about what other people think about what you do. I'd like you to meditate about any changes that you feel will serve you. Do this now while I am quiet for a while.

(Pause for two and a half minutes.)

Are you going to make changes?

(Pause for ten seconds.)

What can you do this week to set these changes into play? (Pause for forty seconds.)

All right . . . you have the power and ability to create your own reality . . . to change what isn't working and to manifest what you desire.

In just a moment I'm going to wake you up. On the count of five, you will open your eyes and be wide awake, fully alert, thinking and acting with calm self-assurance. You'll awaken feeling as if you've just taken a relaxing nap, and you'll be at peace with yourself, the world, and everyone in it.

Number one, coming on up now and feeling an expanding spiritual light within.

Number two, coming up, feeling at peace with all life.

Number three, coming on up and tapping into an internal balance and harmony.

Number four, recall the situation in the room.

Number five, wide awake, wide awake. Open your eyes and feel good. Number five, wide awake.

Answers from Spirit

This induction process is designed to receive answers from Spirit.

You're breathing deeply and relaxing completely.

Breathing deeply and relaxing completely ... and allowing a quietness of spirit to come in. Taking a deep breath in and holding it as long as you comfortably can ... then let the breath out slowly through slightly parted lips, and when the breath is all the way out, push it further out, and further out ... and then repeat the process. Breathing deeply, and when any outside thoughts come into your mind, simply brush them aside and tell yourself, "I'll deal with that later," and then return your concentration to the sound of my voice, and breathing deeply and relaxing completely.

And in just a moment I'm going to relax your body one part at a time. So play the role, play the part and feel your body relaxing as I ask you to do so. And the relaxing power is coming into the toes of both of your feet at the same time ... and it's moving right on down into the balls of your feet, into your arches, into your heels, and right on up to your ankles. Completely relaxed, completely relaxed ... and the relaxing sensations now move on up your legs to your knees, relaxing all the muscles as it goes. And on up your legs now, to your thighs and to your hips. Permeating every cell and every atom.

And you're relaxing completely, relaxing completely, keeping your full attention on the sound of my voice and relaxing your body, as the relaxing sensations move on down into the fingers of both of your hands . . . relaxing your hands. Feel your hands relaxing. And your lower arms are relaxed, and your upper arms are relaxed. Fingers and hands and lower arms and upper arms . . . just completely relaxed.

And the relaxing sensations now move on down into the base of your spine, your root chakra. Imagine a warmth in your root chakra as if a ray of sunlight were coming into the room and falling upon your spine . . . and it feels good. You imagine this warmth now moving up your spine . . . up your spine . . . up your spine and into the back of your neck and shoulder muscles. And your shoulder muscles are now loose and limp . . . loose and limp . . . just completely relaxed.

And the relaxing sensations now move on up the back of your neck and into your scalp. Relaxing your scalp. Feel your scalp relaxing, and feel the relaxing sensations now drain down into your facial muscles, relaxing your facial muscles. Your jaw is relaxed. Allow a little space between your teeth. And your throat is relaxed. Your entire body is now relaxed all over in every way. And all tension is gone from your body and mind.

And we're now going to balance and energize your aura and attune you to the subtle vibrations that support the perception of subjective awareness.

So to begin, imagine a beam of iridescent white light coming down from above and entering your crown chakra of spirituality on the top of your head. Imagine the light . . . create it with the unlimited power of your mind. This is the Universal light of life energy, and you feel it stimulating this chakra center, which is purple in color. Visualize a swirling vortex of purple and the light opens, balances, and charges this chakra center. Imagine the opening, balancing, charging.

(Pause for five seconds.)

The light is now moving on down into the center of your forehead: your brow chakra, which is a swirling blue-violet vortex of energy. Perceive the blue-violet color, and feel the balancing and energizing that is taking place here.

Opening, balancing, energizing.

(Pause for five seconds.)

And the light is now moving on down into your throat chakra, which is a swirling, silvery-blue vortex of energy.

Perceive the silvery-blue color, and feel the balancing and energizing that is taking place here. Opening, balancing, energizing.

(Pause for five seconds.)

And the light is now moving on down into your heart chakra, which is to be perceived as a golden glow. Perceive the golden color, and feel the balancing and energizing of your heart chakra center. Opening, balancing, energizing.

(Pause for five seconds.)

And the light is now moving on down into your solar plexus chakra, located at the level of your navel. This chakra is to be visualized as several shades of red in color. Perceive the red colors, and imagine the balancing and energizing that is taking place here. Opening, balancing, energizing.

(Pause for five seconds.)

And the light is moving on down into your sacral or spleen chakra, which is located a little below your navel. This swirling vortex of energy is a rainbow of colors. Perceive the many colors and feel the balancing and energizing that is taking place here. Opening, balancing, energizing.

(Pause for five seconds.)

And the light is now moving on down into your root chakra at the base of your spine. This chakra is to be visualized as a swirling vortex of energy, red and orange in color. Perceive the reds and oranges, and feel the balancing and energizing that is taking place here. Opening, balancing, energizing.

(Pause for five seconds.)

And your chakras are opened, balanced, and charged, thus expanding your aura and attuning you to the subtle vibrations that support the perception of subjective awareness.

And it's now time to imagine the bright white light moving back up into heart area. Visualize your heart center overflowing with the Universal light of life energy.

And now imagine the light emerging from your heart center to surround your body in a protective aura of bright white God light.

And you are totally protected. Totally protected. Only your own Guides and Masters or highly evolved and loving entities who mean you well will be able to influence you in any way in this altered state of consciousness session.

As you continue to focus upon the sound of my voice, I am going to count you down, down, down ... so vividly imagine yourself in a situation going down ... walking down stairs, downhill, down the side of a pyramid ... or any situation in which you see yourself going down, while I count backwards from seven to one.

Number seven, deeper, deeper, deeper, down, down, down.

Number six, deeper, deeper, deeper, down, down, down. Number five, deeper, deeper, deeper, down, down, down. Number four, deeper, deeper, deeper, down, down, down. Number three, deeper, deeper, deeper, down, down, down.

Number two, deeper, deeper, deeper, down, down, down. Number one, deeper, deeper, deeper, down, down, down.

And you're relaxed and at ease, and you feel deep. But let's go down a little deeper now ... deeper now.

Number seven, deeper, deeper, deeper, down, down, down.

Number six, deeper, deeper, deeper, down, down, down. Number five, deeper, deeper, deeper, down, down, down. Number four, deeper, deeper, deeper, down, down, down. Number three, deeper, deeper, deeper, down, down, down.

Number two, deeper, deeper, deeper, down, down, down. Number one, deeper, deeper, deeper, down, down, down.

And you are now completely relaxed and at ease. And if you feel uncomfortable at any time, you can easily bring yourself up by counting up from one to five and saying the words, "Wide awake."

You're relaxed and at ease . . . and a quietness of spirit permeates your body and mind. And it's time to call in those on the other side in Spirit who love you, and watch over you, and teach you. So call out silently in your mind. Ask your Spirit Guides, your Master teachers, and those who have crossed over but once loved you in life, to come to you and be with you now . . . all you have to do is ask. Hear your voice calling out to those who support you in spirit . . . hear your voice echo out across the Universe and back to you . . . asking those who love, teach, and guide you to be here now, to assist you to find answers. Call out silently. Ask.

(Pause for thirty seconds)

And your Guides and Masters and loved ones are now here with you. And they have the power and ability to communicate awareness to you—to sharing inspiring words to surface in your mind. To receive this wisdom, all you have to do is trust and allow words to form as sentences. If you want, you can open your eyes and quickly write them down . . . and then close your eyes and await the next question.

All right . . . we'll begin by asking those in spirit to send you one sentence relating to your career. What is the one sentence relating to your career that would be of most value for you to receive at this time? On the count of three, this important sentence will form in your mind. Number one, number two, and number three.

(Pause for forty-five seconds.)

All right, let go of this, and it's now time for those in Spirit to share some new awareness in the form of a sentence that refers to any career changes or new directions that would be of value for you to become aware of. Career changes or new directions. Trust the sentence that forms in your mind on the count of three. Number one, number two, and number three.

(Pause for forty-five seconds.)

OK, it's time to move on and ask those in Spirit to provide you with a sentence that would be of most value in regard to increasing your income. Trust this sentence about increasing your income to come in on the count of three.

Number one, number two, and number three.

(Pause for forty-five seconds.)

All right, letting go, remembering, and moving on to ask those in Spirit to provide you with a sentence that would be of most value in regard to your goals for the future. Trust the sentence that comes into your mind regarding your goals.

Number one, number two and number three.

(Pause for forty-five seconds.)

And the flow of energy between you and those in Spirit is intensifying as you continue to perceive valuable information. And now, if there is an area of your life where restrictive thinking is acting against you, allow an understanding of this restriction to form as a sentence on the count of three.

Number one, number two, and number three.

(Pause for forty-five seconds.)

And we're now going to move on to perceive a sentence relating to your key relationship . . . and if you don't have a primary relationship, but are seeking one, this sentence will relate to your quest. So allow a sentence, the most important sentence about your relationship, to form in your mind, on the count of three. Number one, number two, and number three.

(Pause for forty-five seconds.)

All right, remember the sentence, but let's move on and explore the area of sex and sexual fulfillment. Those in Spirit will now provide you with a sentence that will be of most value for you to receive in regard to sex. The sentence will form in your mind on the count of three. Number one, number two, and number three.

(Pause for forty-five seconds.)

OK, the next area of exploration is in regard to friends and/or family. Those who care for you on the other side will send you an important sentence regarding friends and or family associates that will form in your mind on the count of three. Number one, number two, and number three.

(Pause for forty-five seconds.)

And it's time to move on as the energy between you and Spirit continues to intensify. You are now to become aware of any soul callings that are taking place. Is your soul calling you to do something in your life? If so you'll perceive an important sentence about soul callings on the count of three. Number one, number two, and number three.

(Pause for forty-five seconds.)

OK . . . it's time to explore your health. Those who love, teach, and guide you on the other side will send you an important sentence regarding your health on the count of three. Number one, number two, and number three.

(Pause for forty-five seconds.)

All right, let's explore your diet and lifestyle. Do you need to make any changes in your diet or lifestyle? If so, a sentence will form in your mind on the count of three.

Number one, number two, and number three.

(Pause for forty-five seconds.)

OK . . . is there an area of your life where you need to establish more clarity as to what is really going on—clarity as to what someone else is up to or clarity of intent in regard to what you really want? So open now and perceive a sentence relating to clarity on the count of three. Number one, number two, and number three.

(Pause for forty-five seconds.)

And as you continue to perceive awareness from Spirit, you sense the increasing intensity of your shared energy connection. And it's now time to explore any area of judgment on your part. Are you judging others in any way that's harmful to your own soul's growth? If so, perceive a sentence relating to judgment on the count of three. Number one, number two, and number three.

(Pause for forty-five seconds.)

OK . . . let's move on to explore your expectations of yourself and others. Do you have expectations that are in conflict with reality—in conflict with what is? If so, you'll perceive an important sentence regarding your expectations on the count of three. Number one, number two, and number three.

(Pause for forty-five seconds.)

All right, it's now time to explore compassion. Is there any area of your life where you need to express more compassion towards others? If so, a sentence will form in your mind on the count of three. Number one, number two, and number three.

(Pause for forty-five seconds.)

And now . . . is there an area in your life that you are trying to control someone else? If so, a sentence will come into your mind on the count of three that will advise you in regard to trying to control. Number one, number two, and number three.

(Pause for forty-five seconds.)

All right, letting go, but remembering everything that you have perceived. And it's now time to become aware of any area of your life that you need to dedicate more time to. Is there an important area of your life you're neglecting and to which you need to provide more time and energy? If so, you'll perceive this awareness on the count of three. Number one, number two, and number three.

(Pause for forty-five seconds.)

OK . . . and it's now time to end this session by perceiving the single most important sentence you could receive at this time. So . . . this most important sentence will form in your mind on the count of three. Number one, number two, and number three.

(Pause for forty-five seconds.)

And now, before awakening, thank those in Spirit who have been sharing with you. Open to their energy and thank them for their assistance, while also remaining alert to any final messages they'd like to share with you.

(Pause for ninety seconds.)

Every day in every way, you become more aware of your connections to Spirit and the value of interacting regularly with those who love, teach, and guide you.

And in just a moment, I'm going to wake you up. On the count of five, you will open your eyes and be wide awake, fully alert, thinking and acting with calm self-assurance. You'll awaken feeling as if you've just taken a relaxing nap, and you'll be at peace with yourself, the world, and everyone in it.

Number one, coming on up now and feeling an expanding spiritual light within.

Number two, coming up feeling at peace with all life.

Number three, coming on up and tapping into internal balance and harmony.

Number four, recall the situation in the room.

And number five, wide awake, wide awake. Open your eyes and feel good. Number five, wide awake.

The Beliefs Process

Beliefs are the basis of reality. Beliefs generate thoughts and emotions, which in turn create all your experiences. It is that simple, and there are no exceptions.

Your beliefs are the result of programming from your current incarnation and your past lives. Many of your beliefs are faulty and self-defeating. They are blocks to your happiness and success. So if you're not satisfied with your life, you need to begin the process of reinvention by changing beliefs.

> *"Belief is an impediment to reality, and that is a very difficult pill to swallow for most of us. We are not seeking reality; we want gratification, and belief gives us gratification, it pacifies us."*
> —J. Krishnamurti

You're breathing deeply and relaxing completely.

Breathing deeply and relaxing completely . . . and allowing a quietness of spirit to come in. Taking a deep breath in and holding it as long as you comfortably can . . . then let the breath out slowly through slightly parted lips, and when the breath is all the way out, push it further out, and further out . . . and then repeat the process. Breathing deeply, and when any outside thoughts come into your mind, simply brush them aside and tell yourself, "I'll deal with that later," and then return your concentration to the sound of my voice, and breathing deeply and relaxing completely.

In just a moment I'm going to relax your body one part at a time. So play the role, play the part, and feel your body relaxing as I ask you to do so. And the relaxing power is coming into the toes of both of your feet at the same time . . . and it's moving right on down into the balls of your feet, into your arches, into your heels, and right on up to your ankles. Completely relaxed, completely relaxed . . . and the relaxing sensations now move on up your legs to your knees, relaxing all the muscles as it goes. And on up your legs now, to your thighs and to your hips. Permeating every cell and every atom.

And you're relaxing completely, relaxing completely, keeping your full attention on the sound of my voice and relaxing your body, as the relaxing sensations move on down into the fingers of both of your hands . . . relaxing your hands. Feel your hands relaxing. And your lower arms are relaxed, and your upper arms are relaxed. Fingers and hands and lower arms and upper arms . . . just completely relaxed.

And the relaxing sensations now move on down into the base of your spine, your root chakra. Imagine a warmth in your root chakra as if a ray of sunlight were coming into the room and falling upon your spine . . . and it feels good. You imagine this warmth now moving up your spine . . . up your spine . . . up your spine and into the back of your

neck and shoulder muscles. And your shoulder muscles are now loose and limp . . . loose and limp . . . just completely relaxed. And the relaxing sensations now move on up the back of your neck and into your scalp. Relaxing your scalp. Feel your scalp relaxing, and feel the relaxing sensations now drain down into your facial muscles, relaxing your facial muscles. Your jaw is relaxed. Allow a little space between your teeth. And your throat is relaxed. Your entire body is now relaxed all over in every way. And all tension is gone from your body and mind.

As you continue to focus upon the sound of my voice, I am going to count you down, down, down . . . so vividly imagine yourself in a situation going down . . . walking down stairs, downhill, down the side of a pyramid . . . or any situation in which you see yourself going down, while I count backwards from seven to one.

Number seven, deeper, deeper, deeper, down, down, down.

Number six, deeper, deeper, deeper, down, down, down.

Number five, deeper, deeper, deeper, down, down, down.

Number four, deeper, deeper, deeper, down, down, down.

Number three, deeper, deeper, deeper, down, down, down.

Number two, deeper, deeper, deeper, down, down, down. Number one, deeper, deeper, deeper, down, down, down.

And you're relaxed and at ease, and you feel deep. But let's go down a little deeper now . . . deeper now.

Number seven, deeper, deeper, deeper, down, down, down.

Number six, deeper, deeper, deeper, down, down, down.

Number five, deeper, deeper, deeper, down, down, down.

Number four, deeper, deeper, deeper, down, down, down.

Number three, deeper, deeper, deeper, down, down, down.

Number two, deeper, deeper, deeper, down, down, down.

Number one, deeper, deeper, deeper, down, down, down.

And you're now relaxed and at ease, and you feel in balance and in harmony. A quietness of spirit permeates your body and mind.

And you have beliefs that are the basis of your reality. These beliefs generate the thoughts and emotions that create all your experiences. So now let's explore some of your general beliefs. I'm going to begin a sentence and I want you to finish it . . . instantly. Don't stop long enough to even think about it. Just instantly, mentally, finish each sentence I begin.

Then take a few moments to look at your emotions in response to each question, for your emotions are generated by your beliefs.

Next, all on your own, if your belief is negative, replace it with a positive belief. All right, now look at your emotions in response to each question. Remember, emotions are generated by your beliefs. If your belief is negative, replace it with a positive belief.

So, let's get started. Here is the first sentence:
(Pause at least twenty-five seconds after each sentence.)
When I think about my body, I feel . . .
When I see someone else who has a perfect body, I . . .
My body is . . .
When I think about exercise, I . . .
My current weight is . . .
People are over the hill when they reach the age of . . .
The older you get, the . . .
Being older means you . . .
When I think about marriage, I . . .
My love relationship is . . .
When I think about communications with my lover, I feel . . .
I know that my personal spiritual truth is . . .
My general belief about powerful people is . . .
In regard to being a woman (or a man), I feel . . .
When I think about masculinity and femininity, I feel . . .
What other people think of me is . . .
I think rich people are . . .
My general belief about money is . . .
In regard to the ego, I think . . .
My general belief about my creative ability is . . .
My general belief about happiness is . . .

All right, now what did I miss? I've covered many aspects of your life, but there are many areas we have not examined. What did I miss? All on your own, I'd like you to explore the beliefs that are not serving you. Explore the areas of your relationships, sexuality, success, spirituality, enlightenment, your body, your health, and your potential to be all you are capable of being.

Do this now while I am quiet for a while.

(Pause for two minutes.)

In just a moment, I'm going to wake you up. On the count of five, you will open your eyes and be wide awake, fully alert, thinking and acting with calm self-assurance. You'll awaken feeling as if you've just taken a relaxing nap, and you'll be at peace with yourself, the world, and everyone in it.

Number one, coming on up now and feeling an expanding spiritual light within.

Number two, coming up feeling at peace with all life.

Number three, coming on up and tapping into an internal balance and harmony.

Number four, recall the situation in the room.

Number five, wide awake, wide awake. Open your eyes and feel good. Number five, wide awake.

The Blue Healing Ray Meditation

You're breathing deeply and relaxing completely.

Breathing deeply and relaxing completely . . . and allowing a quietness of spirit to come in. Taking a deep breath in and holding it as long as you comfortably can . . . then let the breath out slowly through slightly parted lips, and when the breath is all the way out, push it further out, and further out . . . and then repeat the process. Breathing deeply, and when any outside thoughts come into your mind, simply brush them aside and tell yourself, "I'll deal with that later," and then return your concentration to the sound of my voice, and breathing deeply and relaxing completely.

And in just a moment I'm going to relax your body one part at a time. So play the role, play the part, and feel your body relaxing as I ask you to do so. And the relaxing power is coming into the toes of both of your feet at the same time . . . and it's moving right on down into the balls of your feet, into your arches, into your heels, and right on up to your ankles. Completely relaxed, completely relaxed . . . and the relaxing sensations now move on up your legs to your knees, relaxing all the muscles as it goes. And on up your legs now, to your thighs and to your hips. Permeating every cell and every atom.

And you're relaxing completely, relaxing completely, keeping your full attention on the sound of my voice and relaxing your body, as the relaxing sensations move on down into the fingers of both of your hands . . . relaxing your hands. Feel your hands relaxing. And your lower arms are relaxed, and your upper arms are relaxed. Fingers and hands and lower arms and upper arms . . . just completely relaxed.

And the relaxing sensations now move on down into the base of your spine, your root chakra. Imagine a warmth in your root chakra, as if a ray of sunlight were coming into the room and falling upon your spine . . . and it feels good. You imagine this warmth now moving up your spine . . . up your spine . . . up your spine and into the back of your neck and shoulder muscles. And your shoulder muscles are now loose and limp . . . loose and limp . . . just completely relaxed. And the relaxing sensations now move on up the back of your neck and into your scalp. Relaxing your scalp. Feel your scalp relaxing, and feel the relaxing sensations now drain down into your facial muscles, relaxing your facial muscles. Your jaw is relaxed. Allow a little space between your teeth. And your throat is relaxed. Your entire body is now relaxed all over in every way. And all tension is gone from your body and mind.

We're now going to balance and energize your aura and attune you to the subtle vibrations that support the perception of subjective awareness. So to begin, imagine a beam of iridescent white light coming down from above and entering your crown chakra of spirituality on the top of your head. Imagine the light . . . create it with the unlimited power of your mind. This is the Universal light of life energy, and you feel it stimulating this chakra center, which is purple in color. Visualize a swirling vortex of purple, and the light opens, balances, and charges this chakra center. Imagine the opening, balancing, charging.

(Pause for five seconds.)

And the light is now moving on down into the center of your forehead—your brow chakra, which is a swirling blue-violet vortex of energy. Perceive the blue-violet color, and feel the balancing and energizing that is taking place here.

Opening, balancing, energizing.

(Pause for five seconds.)

And the light is now moving on down into your throat chakra, which is a swirling silvery-blue vortex of energy.

Perceive the silvery-blue color, and feel the balancing and energizing that is taking place here. Opening, balancing, energizing.

(Pause for five seconds.)

And the light is now moving on down into your heart chakra, which is to be perceived as a golden glow. Perceive the golden color, and feel the balancing and energizing of your heart chakra center. Opening, balancing, energizing.

(Pause for five seconds.)

And the light is now moving on down into your solar plexus chakra, located at the level of your navel. This chakra is to be visualized as several shades of red in color. Perceive the red colors, and imagine the balancing and energizing that is taking place here. Opening, balancing, energizing.

(Pause for five seconds.)

And the light is moving on down into your sacral or spleen chakra, which is located a little below your navel. This swirling vortex of energy is a rainbow of colors. Perceive the many colors, and feel the balancing and energizing that is taking place here. Opening, balancing, energizing.

(Pause for five seconds.)

And the light is now moving on down into your root chakra at the base of your spine. This chakra is to be visualized as a swirling vortex of energy, red and orange in color. Perceive the reds and oranges, and feel the balancing and energizing that is taking place here. Opening, balancing, energizing.

(Pause for five seconds.)

And your chakras are opened, balanced, and charged, thus expanding your aura and attuning you to the subtle vibrations that support the perception of subjective awareness.

And it's now time to imagine the bright white light moving back up into heart area. Visualize your heart center overflowing with the Universal light of life energy.

And now imagine the light emerging from your heart center to surround your body in a protective aura of bright white God light.

And you are totally protected. Totally protected. Only your own Guides and Masters or highly evolved and loving entities who mean you well will be able to influence you in any way in this altered state of consciousness session.

And as you continue to focus upon the sound of my voice, I am going to count you down, down, down . . . so vividly imagine yourself in a situation going down . . . walking down stairs, downhill, down the side of a pyramid . . . or any situation in which you see yourself going down, while I count backwards from seven to one.

Number seven, deeper, deeper, deeper, down, down, down.

Number six, deeper, deeper, deeper, down, down, down.

Number five, deeper, deeper, deeper, down, down, down.

Number four, deeper, deeper, deeper, down, down, down.

Number three, deeper, deeper, deeper, down, down, down.

Number two, deeper, deeper, deeper, down, down, down.

Number one, deeper, deeper, deeper, down, down, down.

And you're relaxed and at ease, and you feel deep. But let's go down a little deeper now . . . deeper now.

Number seven, deeper, deeper, deeper, down, down, down.

Number six, deeper, deeper, deeper, down, down, down.

Number five, deeper, deeper, deeper, down, down, down.

Number four, deeper, deeper, deeper, down, down, down.

Number three, deeper, deeper, deeper, down, down, down.

Number two, deeper, deeper, deeper, down, down, down.

Number one, deeper, deeper, deeper, down, down, down.

And you are now completely relaxed and at ease. And if you feel uncomfortable at any time, you can easily bring yourself up by counting up from one to five and saying the words, "Wide awake."

And you're now relaxed and at ease, and it's time to vividly imagine a bright blue light—the Divine healing ray—coming down from above and entering your crown chakra of spirituality on the top of your head . . . Create the light with the unlimited power of your mind . . . Imagine the light . . . feel the light within you . . . experience the light.

The blue healing ray now flows through body . . . into your heart . . . nurturing your heart and releasing all tension as it pulses through every cell and every atom . . . permeating your life force with Divine healing light.

And the intense, shimmering, iridescent blue healing light now fills your body to overflowing. Take a few moments to vividly visualize and experience the light.

(Pause for twenty seconds.)

And the light has released all negative blockages, and the healing energy flows through you . . . healing . . . energizing . . . healing . . . energizing. The blue healing ray now courses through your body and mind, releasing your life force . . . healing . . . energizing . . . healing . . . energizing. Your body now has the ability to heal itself if you respond with the proper nourishment, care, treatment, and mental programming. Within you lies a natural healer, and by combining imagery and life-affirming attitude, you can draw upon your untapped potential to manifest physical miracles.

And the following positive suggestions will be communicated to every level of your body and mind, and they will be accepted on every level of your body and mind. You ask it, you beseech it, you mark it . . . and so it is.

Your immune system is in perfect balance.

Your coronary arteries are clear and open, supplying blood, oxygen, and nutrients to your heart.

Your faithful bodyguard cells seek out and contain or destroy any abnormal cells in your body.

The healing light within nourishes your healthy cells.

Your liver functions at full capacity, detoxifying impurities and reactivating the enzymes essential for healthy metabolism.

Your digestive system functions perfectly, fully digesting your food and supplying your system with essential nutrients.

You find it easy to adhere to a diet and lifestyle that supports a healthy body and mind.

You now release all disharmonious emotions and replace them with an accepting, harmonious attitude.

You experience a sense of security and express a positive outlook, which helps you to maintain a healthy body.

Every day in every way, you find it easier to express your feelings and emotions.

You now accept yourself and others without expectations or blame.

You give up the need to manipulate or control anyone else in any way.

You are balanced and harmonious, and every day in every way you become a little healthier.

And these suggestions have been communicated to every level of your body and mind . . . and so it is. You are worthy and deserving of your own highest good, which begins with perfect health. Perfect health.

And it's now time to use visualization to communicate your desires to every level of your body and mind. So vividly imagine yourself in perfect health. Imagine you are fully healed. Experience your reaction and the reaction of others . . . And visualize yourself doing all the things you want to do.

Healed and healthy. Do this now while I am quiet for a while.

(Pause for sixty seconds.)

And you've just seen your own reality. You are healing. You are healed. And your body is filled with the blue healing ray, and you're centered and at peace with yourself, the world, and everyone in it.

And in just a moment, I'm going to wake you up. On the count of five, you will open your eyes and be wide awake, fully alert, thinking and acting with calm self-assurance. You'll awaken feeling as if you've just taken a relaxing nap, and you'll be at peace with yourself, the world, and everyone in it.

Number one, coming on up now and feeling an expanding spiritual light within.

Number two, coming up feeling at peace with all life.

Number three, coming on up and tapping into an internal balance and harmony.

Number four, recall the situation in the room.

And number five, wide awake, wide awake. Open your eyes and feel good. Number five, wide awake.

Buttons

A robot has no choice as to how it acts. It has wiring and circuits, and it is programmed so that when a particular button is pushed, it reacts according to programming. And we react very much the same. We all have buttons, and depending upon which button is pushed, we act like robots. We demonstrate our machineness.

The Buttons Process

You're breathing deeply and relaxing completely.

Breathing deeply and relaxing completely . . . and allowing a quietness of spirit to come in. Taking a deep breath in and holding it as long as you comfortably can . . . then let the breath out slowly through slightly parted lips, and when the breath is all the way out, push it further out, and further out . . . and then repeat the process. Breathing deeply, and when any outside thoughts come into your mind, simply brush them aside and tell yourself, "I'll deal with that later," and then return your concentration to the sound of my voice, and breathing deeply and relaxing completely.

And in just a moment I'm going to relax your body one part at a time. So play the role, play the part, and feel your body relaxing as I ask you to do so. And the relaxing power is coming into the toes of both of your feet at the same time . . . and it's moving right on down into the balls of your feet, into your arches, into your heels, and right on up to your ankles. Completely relaxed, completely relaxed . . . and the relaxing sensations now move on up your legs to your knees, relaxing all the muscles as it goes. And on up your legs now, to your thighs and to your hips. Permeating every cell and every atom.

And you're relaxing completely, relaxing completely, keeping your full attention on the sound of my voice and relaxing your body, as the relaxing sensations move on down into the fingers of both of your hands . . . relaxing your hands. Feel your hands relaxing. And your lower arms are relaxed, and your upper arms are relaxed. Fingers and hands and lower arms and upper arms . . . just completely relaxed.

And the relaxing sensations now move on down into the base of your spine, your root chakra. Imagine a warmth in your root chakra as if a ray of sunlight were coming into the room and falling upon your spine . . . and it feels good. You imagine this warmth now moving up your spine . . . up your spine . . . up your spine and into the back of your neck and shoulder muscles. And your shoulder muscles are now loose and limp . . . loose and limp . . . just completely relaxed. And the relaxing sensations now move on up the back of your neck and into your scalp. Relaxing your scalp. Feel your scalp relaxing, and feel the relaxing sensations now drain down into your facial muscles, relaxing your facial muscles. Your jaw is relaxed. Allow a little space between your teeth. And your throat is relaxed. Your entire body is now relaxed all over in every way. And all tension is gone from your body and mind.

And as you continue to focus upon the sound of my voice, I am going to count you down, down, down . . . so vividly imagine yourself in a situation going down . . . walking down stairs, downhill, down the side of a pyramid . . . or any situation in which you see yourself going down, while I count backwards from seven to one.

Number seven, deeper, deeper, deeper, down, down, down.

Number six, deeper, deeper, deeper, down, down, down.

Number five, deeper, deeper, deeper, down, down, down.

Number four, deeper, deeper, deeper, down, down, down.

Number three, deeper, deeper, deeper, down, down, down.

Number two, deeper, deeper, deeper, down, down, down.

Number one, deeper, deeper, deeper, down, down, down.

And you're relaxed and at ease, and you feel deep. But let's go down a little deeper now . . . deeper now.

Number seven, deeper, deeper, deeper, down, down, down.

Number six, deeper, deeper, deeper, down, down, down.

Number five, deeper, deeper, deeper, down, down, down.

Number four, deeper, deeper, deeper, down, down, down.

Number three, deeper, deeper, deeper, down, down, down.

Number two, deeper, deeper, deeper, down, down, down.

Number one, deeper, deeper, deeper, down, down, down.

And you are now completely relaxed and at ease. And if you feel uncomfortable at any time, you can easily bring yourself up by counting up from one to five and saying the words, "Wide awake."

And you're now relaxed and at ease and centered upon achieving your goals. You're at peace and feel in balance and harmony, and a quietness of spirit permeates your body and mind.

And it's time to explore some of your past programming.

We all have buttons connected to our computerlike subconscious mind. When these buttons are pushed, we demonstrate our machineness by reacting with emotion— often anger, repression or fear.

So in this process, we're going to explore what pushes your reaction buttons—what causes you to react. The idea is to be straight with yourself and to trust the very first thought that comes into your mind. OK, here's the first question:

In your personal life, what pushes your buttons causing you to quickly become angry, or you repress, or become fearful?

(Pause for twenty seconds.)

What is the first occupational or career button that comes to mind—when it gets pushed, you become upset, or you repress, or you experience fear?

(Pause for twenty seconds.)

What pushes your embarrassment buttons?

(Pause for twenty seconds.)

What public, national, or international situation pushes your buttons, causing you to be angry, to repress or experience fear?

(Pause for twenty seconds.)

What does the person closest to you do to push your buttons?

(Pause for twenty seconds.)

How does what other people think push your buttons?

(Pause for twenty seconds.)

All right, now for a few moments, meditate upon how what other people think about you is manipulating you. What your mate or lover thinks . . . your friends, your coworkers, your children, and your parents. Are they pushing your buttons, causing you to be the way they want you to be? Meditate all on your own.

(Pause for ninety seconds.)

OK, can you get that you've been programmed, brainwashed, from birth to worry about what other people think? You grew up worrying about what others thought about you. Your parents worried about what other people thought.

But what others think may not be in your best interest. Maybe what *you* think is what's most important.

In most areas of life, there is no such thing as moral and immoral, right and wrong, ethical and unethical. A group of people agree upon terminology, and maybe they agree to call a particular action or practice wrong, but that does not make it wrong. That doesn't change what it actually is.

Right, wrong, moral, immoral, ethical, unethical, are all concepts, which in fact exist only by agreement of a group of people. That does not make it right or wrong . . . only what we call right or wrong. It doesn't change what it actually is. In living in a society, we must be willing to accept the consequences of our actions in regard to the laws of society. Yet most of the conflicts with the opinions of other people are not legal issues. It may be ill-advised for you to allow what other people think to push your reaction buttons and repress who you really are.

Another thing: The people in your life quickly learn about your buttons, and they use them to manipulate you. And that reduces your personal power. I would like you to meditate upon all this and to consider any changes you want to make in your life.

(Pause for two minutes.)

You no longer have to be a robot that reacts to past programming that doesn't serve you. You have the power and ability to create your own reality . . . to change what isn't working and to manifest what you desire.

And in just a moment, I'm going to wake you up. On the count of five, you will open your eyes and be wide awake, fully alert, thinking and acting with calm self-assurance. You'll awaken feeling as if you've just taken a relaxing nap, and you'll be at peace with yourself, the world, and everyone in it.

Number one, coming on up now and feeling an expanding spiritual light within.

Number two, coming up feeling at peace with all life.

Number three, coming on up and tapping into an internal balance and harmony.

Number four, recall the situation in the room.

And number five, wide awake, wide awake. Open your eyes and feel good. Number five, wide awake.

Chakras

The chakras are the seven energy centers of the etheric body. Dick Sutphen did not use the rainbow chakra colors that are commonly used today. He used the colors as given in the teachings of the Theosophical Society.

The crown chakra is on the top of the head. This chakra of spirituality is violet or purple in color and is linked to the pineal gland. To fully awaken your crown chakra, you must balance body, mind, and spirit.

The third eye or brow chakra is located in the center of our forehead. Blue-violet in color, it is the seat of your mind, representing thought, intuition, and the ability to manifest reality. Physically, it is associated with your pineal and pituitary glands, plus your eyes, ears, nose, and sinuses.

The throat chakra is silvery-blue in color and is a carrier wave of basic elements and the sense of sound and voice. Physically it relates to communications. It is associated with the vocal cords and regulates metabolism.

The heart chakra is golden in color and deals with the development of compassion and the emotions that bind people. It also represents the qualities of air in your personality and the physical sense of touch.

The solar plexus chakra is located at the level of your navel, is many shades of red in color and represents fire in your personality, including issues of personal power. Physically, the chakra relates to your digestive system. It also supplies subtle energy to most of the major organs, including the stomach, pancreas, liver, gall bladder, and spleen.

The sacral or spleen chakra is located below your navel and is to be visualized as a rainbow of colors. This chakra is associated with sexuality. Physically it relates to the testes and ovaries as well as the intestinal tract and colon.

The root chakra is located at the base of the spine and is red and orange in color. It's associated with your creative energies and survival instincts. It also relates to how grounded you are in your activities.

Before conducting this session, you should learn more about why you would link two people's top chakras and the benefits such a link could have. Listening to Dick's audio course *Chakra Link* is highly recommended. Dick oftentimes used this session for couples who came to him looking for answers in their union together. This was a way for the couples to understand what their partner was thinking and feeling on a much deeper level. Often you will direct the partner to go back to a lifetime that the two shared, allowing each to explore the same lifetime from differing perspectives.

Once the chakra connections are made, you can take one of the partners into a past-life regression, while the other partner will tag along, usually mentally experiencing any emotions associated with the lifetime or event. Or you can use this chakra link to simply remain quiet and totally open to visions, impressions, concepts. You can then later compare your perceptions. The potentials of the chakra link are unlimited.

The Chakra Connection

This is used to link two individuals before a full hypnosis session. It is done to have the subjects see and feel what the other is experiencing.

You will use your client's names instead of "A" and "B."

An intense psychic connection can be established between two people by conducting a chakra visualization exercise. You will only connect the top four chakras.

Lie down side by side, hold hands, and do your deep breathing.

We are now going to visualize a connection taking place between the crown chakras at the top of our heads. Visualize an intense violet light emanating from the top of your head . . . see it in your mind . . . it is arching out, up, across, and over to connect with my head. Make it real with the unlimited power of your mind. It is an intense, shimmering, iridescent violet light connecting our crown chakras. (Pause.) The connection is now complete.

Both people participate in the visualization, and the process continues with the next three chakras:

The third eye, brow chakra, in the center of your forehead, is blue-violet in color.

The throat chakra: silvery-blue in color.

The heart chakra: golden in color.

With practice, many couples are capable of perceiving identical impressions, emotions, or regression experiences in an altered state of consciousness.

Make sure you dissolve the connection at the end of the session by going through the same process, only stating, "The connection is dissolved," starting with the heart chakra and continuing up to the crown chakra.

The Chakra Link Session

It's now time to experience this chakra link meditation, which is structured for two people to experience together. It's an exercise in sending and receiving.

Decide which of you will be the sender (A) and which will be the receiver (B). Then lie down or sit back side by side, and touch or hold hands to intensify the link. The session will begin with a body relaxation, in which you are to imagine each part of your body relaxing as I ask you to do so.

Mentally project relaxing sensations into each area of your body in response to my words. This will be followed by a chakra balancing and energizing exercise that will expand your aura so that you're more receptive to subjective perception. During the chakra balancing exercise, vividly imagine the colors as swirling vortexes of energy in each of the seven chakra centers.

Please understand that unless you're conditioned and work in an altered state, it will take you about two weeks of doing a session every day to attain your natural level—the level at which you will most effectively experience the session.

So now make sure you won't be interrupted, then make yourself comfortable lying down or sitting up. Take two to three minutes of deep breathing. Breathe in through your nose, hold for as long as you comfortably can, then let it out slowly through slightly parted lips.

(Pause for two to three minutes.)

You're breathing deeply and relaxing completely.

Breathing deeply and relaxing completely . . . and allowing a quietness of spirit to come in. Taking a deep breath in and holding it as long as you comfortably can . . . then let the breath out slowly through slightly parted lips, and when the breath is all the way out, push it further out, and further out . . . and then repeat the process. Breathing deeply, and when any outside thoughts come into your mind, simply brush them aside and tell yourself, "I'll deal with that later," and then return your concentration to the sound of my voice, and breathing deeply and relaxing completely.

And in just a moment I'm going to relax your body one part at a time. So play the role, play the part, and feel your body relaxing as I ask you to do so. And the relaxing power is coming into the toes of both of your feet at the same time . . . and it's moving right on down into the balls of your feet, into your arches, into your heels, and right on up to your ankles. Completely relaxed, completely relaxed . . . and the relaxing sensations now move on up your legs to your knees, relaxing all the muscles as they go. And on up your legs now, to your thighs and to your hips. Permeating every cell and every atom.

And you're relaxing completely, relaxing completely, keeping your full attention on the sound of my voice and relaxing your body, as the relaxing sensations move on down into the fingers of both of your hands . . . relaxing your hands. Feel your hands relaxing. And your lower arms are relaxed, and your upper arms are relaxed. Fingers and hands and lower arms and upper arms . . . just completely relaxed.

And the relaxing sensations now move on down into the base of your spine, your root chakra. Imagine a warmth in your root chakra as if a ray of sunlight were coming into the room and falling upon your spine . . . and it feels good. You imagine this warmth now moving up your spine . . . up your spine . . . up your spine and into the back of your neck and shoulder muscles. And your shoulder muscles are now loose and limp . . . loose and limp . . . just completely relaxed.

And the relaxing sensations now move on up the back of your neck and into your scalp. Relaxing your scalp. Feel your scalp relaxing, and feel the relaxing sensations now drain down into your facial muscles, relaxing your facial muscles. Your jaw is relaxed. Allow a little space between your teeth. And your throat is relaxed. Your entire body is now relaxed all over in every way. And all tension is gone from your body and mind.

And we're now going to balance and energize your aura and attune you to the subtle vibrations that support the perception of subjective awareness. So to begin, imagine a beam of iridescent white light coming down from above and entering your crown chakra of spirituality on the top of your head. Imagine the light . . . create it with the unlimited power of your mind. This is the Universal light of life energy, and you feel it stimulating this chakra center, which is purple in color. Visualize a swirling vortex of purple and the light opens, balances, and charges this chakra center. Imagine the opening, balancing, charging.

(Pause for five seconds.)

And the light is now moving on down into the center of your forehead—your brow chakra, which is a swirling blue-violet vortex of energy. Perceive the blue-violet color, and feel the balancing and energizing that is taking place here.

Opening, balancing, energizing.

(Pause for five seconds.)

And the light is now moving on down into your throat chakra, which is a swirling silvery-blue vortex of energy.

Perceive the silvery-blue color, and feel the balancing and energizing that is taking place here. Opening, balancing, energizing.

(Pause for five seconds.)

And the light is now moving on down into your heart chakra, which is to be perceived as a golden glow. Perceive the golden color, and feel the balancing and energizing of your heart chakra center. Opening, balancing, energizing.

(Pause for five seconds.)

And the light is now moving on down into your solar plexus chakra, located at the level of your navel. This chakra is to be visualized as several shades of red in color. Perceive the red colors, and imagine the balancing and energizing that is taking place here. Opening, balancing, energizing.

(Pause for five seconds.)

And the light is moving on down into your sacral or spleen chakra, which is located a little below your navel. This swirling vortex of energy is a rainbow of colors. Perceive the many colors and feel the balancing and energizing that is taking place here. Opening, balancing, energizing.

(Pause for five seconds.)

And the light is now moving on down into your root chakra at the base of your spine. This chakra is to be visualized as a swirling vortex of energy, red and orange in color. Perceive the reds and oranges, and feel the balancing and energizing that is taking place here. Opening, balancing, energizing.

(Pause for five seconds.)

And your chakras are opened, balanced, and charged, thus expanding your aura and attuning you to the subtle vibrations that support the perception of subjective awareness.

And it's now time to imagine the bright white light moving back up into heart area. Visualize your heart center overflowing with the Universal light of life energy.

And now imagine the light emerging from your heart center to surround your body in a protective aura of bright white God light.

And you are totally protected. Totally protected. Only your own Guides and Masters or highly evolved and loving entities who mean you well will be able to influence you in any way in this altered state of consciousness session.

And as you continue to focus upon the sound of my voice, I am going to count you down, down, down . . . so vividly imagine yourself in a situation going down . . . walking down stairs, downhill, down the side of a pyramid . . . or any situation in which you see yourself going down, while I count backwards from seven to one.

Number seven, deeper, deeper, deeper, down, down, down.

Number six, deeper, deeper, deeper, down, down, down.

Number five, deeper, deeper, deeper, down, down, down.

Number four, deeper, deeper, deeper, down, down, down.

Number three, deeper, deeper, deeper, down, down, down.

Number two, deeper, deeper, deeper, down, down, down.

Number one, deeper, deeper, deeper, down, down, down.

And you're relaxed and at ease, and you feel deep. But let's go down a little deeper now . . . deeper now.

Number seven, deeper, deeper, deeper, down, down, down.

Number six, deeper, deeper, deeper, down, down, down.

Number five, deeper, deeper, deeper, down, down, down.

Number four, deeper, deeper, deeper, down, down, down.

Number three, deeper, deeper, deeper, down, down, down.

Number two, deeper, deeper, deeper, down, down, down.

Number one, deeper, deeper, deeper, down, down, down.

You are relaxed and at ease, side by side, and holding hands or simply just touching one another . . . and it's time to begin to establish a psychic connection by linking the top four energy chakras. And we'll begin having you imagine a deep purple light emitting from the crown chakra on the top of your head and arching up, out, and over to connect with the crown chakra of your partner beside you . . . see it very, very vividly. A violet-purple arch of light connecting the two of you. See it . . . create it with your mind, and the connection becomes your reality.

(Pause for ten seconds.)

And the connection is now complete. And it's time to imagine a blue-violet light emitting from your third eye chakra in the middle of your forehead and arching up, out, and over to connect with the third eye chakra of your partner beside you . . . see it very, very vividly. A blue-violet light connecting the two of you. See it . . . create it in your mind, and the connection becomes your reality.

(Pause for ten seconds.)

And the connection is now complete. And it's time to imagine a silvery-blue light emitting from your throat chakra arching up, out, and over to connect with the throat chakra of your partner beside you . . . see it very, very vividly. A silvery-blue light connecting the two of you. See it . . . create it in your mind, and the connection becomes your reality.

(Pause for ten seconds.)

And the connection is now complete. And it's time to imagine a golden light emitting from your heart chakra in the middle of your forehead and arching up, out, and over to connect with the heart chakra of your partner beside you . . . see it very, very vividly. A golden light connecting the two of you. See it . . . create it in your mind, and the connection becomes your reality.

(Pause for ten seconds.)

The connection is now complete . . . and from this moment on, you will each be able to perceive what the other perceives . . . feel what the other feels . . . and know what's in the other's mind. You've combined your energies. Take a few moments to experience the chakra link . . . two minds and two spirits psychically connected . . . a mental and spiritual union.

(Pause for forty-five seconds.)

And we're now going to explore your extrasensory powers with some sending and receiving exercises. You will remember everything you send and everything you receive. And I suggest that as B, you will trust the very first impression—your immediate thought.

All right, A, on the count of three, you are to send a visual image combined with an emotion to B. As an example, you might send an image of yourself giving B a hug. Combine this with an emotion appropriate to your relationship . . . so take a moment to decide what you're going to send—an image combined with an emotion.

(Pause for thirty seconds.)

All right, now A, on the count of three you will mentally focus all your energy upon this image and emotion. B, on the count of three, you are to receive the impressions from A. Trust what comes into your mind.

Number one . . . number two . . . and number three.

(Pause for forty-five seconds.)

And B, you should now be aware of the impressions, and it's your turn to send an image and an emotion to A. So take a few moments to decide what you're going to send.

(Pause for thirty seconds.) OK, on the count of three, B, you will focus all your energy upon the image and emotion. A, you will perceive what B is sending you. Trust your first impression.

Number one . . . number two . . . and number three.

(Pause for forty-five seconds.)

All right, now remember what you sent and what you received. And now, A you're to send B a primary color on the count of three. Send red, blue, or yellow. Send it on the count of three.

Number one . . . number two . . . and number three.

(Pause for fifteen seconds.)

OK, now B, you're to send A a primary color on the count of three. Send red, blue, or yellow.

Number one . . . number two . . . and number three.

(Pause for fifteen seconds.)

All right, we're now going to move on into another area of sending and receiving. A, I am going to move you back into the past. Way, way back to one of your previous incarnations to explore a positive experience from that lifetime. You will perceive this past-life event as an observer. And B, you will perceive what A is experiencing.

OK, A, be open to every thought, feeling, or visualization that comes into your mind . . .

And it's time to imagine a tunnel leading back into your past. It can be any kind of tunnel from a tunnel through clouds to a subway tunnel . . . but make it real . . . and in just a moment I'll begin counting you through this tunnel to your past. I'll count from five to one as you imagine yourself moving back into your past . . . through the tunnel to a light way down at the end. And on the count of one, you'll step out of the end of the tunnel, and impressions will begin to come in.

So step into the tunnel.

Number five, beginning to move back in time. Feel it happening, allow it to happen. You're letting go of the present and moving back in time.

Number four, feel it happening . . . feel yourself moving through the tunnel toward the light way down at the end. Visualize the light. Back in time. And on the count of one, you'll vividly imagine a situation in the past.

Number three, moving back in time to the date and location and to something that happened at that time. Moving through the tunnel, toward the light, getting closer and closer now.

Number two, you're almost there, and on the next count, you'll step out of the end of the tunnel, and you'll make up thoughts or feelings or impressions to imagine what a past life there might have been like.

Number one. You are now there. Step out and allow impressions to come in. Vividly imagine the environment. What are you doing? What is happening?

Are you outdoors or indoors? Your mind knows . . . and if the impressions are not yet clear, simply choose one or the other.

(Pause for five seconds.)

If you're outdoors, imagine the environment. Are you in the woods, the prairie, or the seaside? Or maybe you're in a town or village or a city. And if you're indoors, look around the room. Is there any furniture? What about windows? How big is the room? . . . Decide . . . and if necessary, just make it up to get the impressions rolling.

(Pause for ten seconds.)

All right . . . are you male or female? Again, your mind knows. Male or female?

(Pause for five seconds.)

And what are you doing at this time?

(Pause for ten seconds)

Is there anyone else there with you?

(Pause for five seconds.)

OK . . . you know if you're outdoors or indoors and if you're male or female . . . and now, on the count of three, look down, and see what you're wearing on your feet. One, two, three. Are you wearing boots, or shoes, or moccasins, or maybe you're barefoot?

(Pause for five seconds.)

And now, if you haven't already done so, it's time to step outside of yourself and perceive what you look like. One, two, three.

(Pause for five seconds.)

What are you wearing? Examine your hair color and styling. Look closely.

(Pause for ten seconds.)

Let's explore the year you're currently experiencing within. The numbers of the year will simply come into your mind as I ask you to perceive them.

OK . . . the first number of the year is (pause) . . . second number (pause) . . . third number (pause) . . . and if there is a fourth number, perceive it now (pause). And is this BC or AD? (pause) . . . and you should now have the year.

Now what about the country or the geographical location you find yourself experiencing within? If necessary, allow the letters of the name of the country or location to come into your mind, one at a time.

(Pause for ten seconds.)

And you should now have the name of the country or location you're experiencing within.

And it's time to let go of this and move forward to a very important situation that will transpire in your future in this lifetime you're now examining. As I count from one to three, time will pass and you'll grow older . . . a few months, years, or many, many years will have passed . . . and it will be the time of something important in your life. One, two, three.

OK, let go of this now and come back to the present. On the count of three, you'll remain with your eyes closed, in a relaxing altered state of consciousness, but back in the present, remembering everything you just experienced.

Number one . . . number two . . . and number three.

All right, now both of you are to remember what you perceived, but now it's B's turn to move back into the past. Way, way back to one of your previous incarnations to explore a positive experience from that lifetime. You will perceive this past-life event as an observer. A, you will perceive what B is experiencing.

OK, B, be open to every thought, feeling, or visualization that comes into your mind.

And it's time to imagine a tunnel leading back into your past. It can be any kind of tunnel from a tunnel through clouds to a subway tunnel . . . but make it real . . . and in just a moment I'll begin counting you through this tunnel to your past. I'll count from five to one as you imagine yourself moving back into your past . . . through the tunnel to a light way down at the end. And on the count of one, you'll step out of the end of the tunnel, and impressions will begin to come in.

So step into the tunnel . . .

Number five, beginning to move back in time. Feel it happening, allow it to happen. You're letting go of the present and moving back in time.

Number four, feel it happening . . . feel yourself toward the light way down at the end. Visualize the light. Back in time.

And on the count of one, you'll vividly imagine a situation in the past.

Number three, moving back in time to the date and location and to something that happened at that time. Moving through the tunnel, toward the light, getting closer and closer now.

Number two, you're almost there, and on the next count, you'll step out of the end of the tunnel, and you'll make up thoughts or feelings or impressions to imagine what a past life there might have been like.

Number one. You are now there. Step out and allow impressions to come in. Vividly imagine the environment. What are you doing? What is happening?

Are you outdoors or indoors? Your mind knows . . . and if the impressions are not yet clear, simply choose one or the other.

(Pause for five seconds.)

If you're outdoors, imagine the environment. Are you in the woods, the prairie, or the seaside? Or maybe you're in a town or village or a city. And if you're indoors, look around the room. Is there any furniture . . . what about windows? How big is the room? . . . Decide . . . and if necessary, just make it up to get the impressions rolling.

(Pause for ten seconds.)

All right . . . are you male or female? Again, your mind knows. Male or female?

(Pause for five seconds.)

And what are you doing at this time?

(Pause for ten seconds.)

Is there anyone else there with you?

(Pause for five seconds.)

OK . . . you know if you're outdoors or indoors and if you're male or female . . . and now, on the count of three, look down and see what you're wearing on your feet. One, two, three. Are you wearing boots, or shoes, or moccasins, or maybe you're barefoot?

(Pause for five seconds.)

And now, if you haven't already done so, it's time to step outside of yourself and perceive what you look like. One, two, three.

(Pause for five seconds.)

What are you wearing? Examine your hair color and styling. Look closely.

(Pause for ten seconds.)

Let's explore the year you're currently experiencing within. The numbers of the year will simply come into your mind as I ask you to perceive them.

OK . . . the first number of the year is (pause) . . . second number (pause) . . . third number (pause) . . . and if there is a fourth number, perceive it now (pause). And is this BC or AD? (pause) . . . and you should now have the year.

Now what about the country or the geographical location you find yourself experiencing within? If necessary, allow the letters of the name of the country or location to come into your mind, one at a time.

(Pause for ten seconds.)

And you should now have the name of the country or location you're experiencing within.

And it's time to let go of this and move forward to a very important situation that will transpire in your future in this lifetime you're now examining. As I count from one to three, time will pass and you'll grow older . . . a few months, years, or many, many years will have passed . . . and it will be the time of something important in your life. One, two, three.

OK, let go of this now and come back to the present. On the count of three, you'll remain with your eyes closed in a relaxing altered state of consciousness, but back in the present, remembering everything you just experienced.

Number one . . . number two . . . and number three.

And again, you will both remember what you perceived during these past-life experiences. And it's now time to open to any awareness that will serve you both at this point in time. Just quiet your mind, be open, and perceive the thoughts, feelings, and impressions that come in to your mind on the count of three. Number one . . . number two . . . and number three.

(Pause for one minute. If your session ends here, go through the process to unlink the heart, throat, third eye, and crown chakras.)

And now it is time to dissolve the chakra connections, beginning with your heart chakra. See the golden light release from your partner's heart chakra and dissolve . . . and so it is. And now the throat chakra . . . see the silvery-blue light release from your partner's throat chakra and dissolve. And the blue-violet light from your third eye chakra is lifting from your partner's chakra and is now dissolved. And now see the violet-purple light emitting from your crown chakras leave your partner's crown and dissolve . . . and so it is. Your chakra link connection is now dissolved. You will remember everything you experienced in this chakra link meditation session, but now it is time to come back to the present.

(Return to the present and awaken.)

Color Therapy

(Play soothing music in the background for this session.)

You're breathing deeply and relaxing completely.

Breathing deeply and relaxing completely... and allowing a quietness of spirit to come in. Taking a deep breath in and holding it as long as you comfortably can ... then let the breath out slowly through slightly parted lips, and when the breath is all the way out, push it further out, and further out ... and then repeat the process. Breathing deeply, and when any outside thoughts come into your mind, simply brush them aside and tell yourself, "I'll deal with that later," and then return your concentration to the sound of my voice, and breathing deeply and relaxing completely.

And in just a moment I'm going to relax your body one part at a time. So play the role, play the part, and feel your body relaxing as I ask you to do so. And the relaxing power is coming into the toes of both of your feet at the same time ... and it's moving right on down into the balls of your feet, into your arches, into your heels and right on up to your ankles. Completely relaxed, completely relaxed ... and the relaxing sensations now move on up your legs to your knees, relaxing all the muscles as it goes. And on up your legs now, to your thighs and to your hips. Permeating every cell and every atom.

And you're relaxing completely, relaxing completely, keeping your full attention on the sound of my voice and relaxing your body, as the relaxing sensations move on down into the fingers of both of your hands . . . relaxing your hands. Feel your hands relaxing. And your lower arms are relaxed, and your upper arms are relaxed. Fingers and hands and lower arms and upper arms . . . just completely relaxed.

And the relaxing sensations now move on down into the base of your spine, your root chakra. Imagine a warmth in your root chakra as if a ray of sunlight were coming into the room and falling upon your spine . . . and it feels good. You imagine this warmth now moving up your spine . . . up your spine . . . up your spine and into the back of your neck and shoulder muscles. And your shoulder muscles are now loose and limp . . . loose and limp . . . just completely relaxed. And the relaxing sensations now move on up the back of your neck and into your scalp. Relaxing your scalp. Feel your scalp relaxing, and feel the relaxing sensations now drain down into your facial muscles, relaxing your facial muscles. Your jaw is relaxed. Allow a little space between your teeth. And your throat is relaxed. Your entire body is now relaxed all over in every way. And all tension is gone from your body and mind.

And we're now going to balance and energize your aura and attune you to the subtle vibrations that support the perception of subjective awareness. So to begin, imagine a beam of iridescent white light coming down from above and entering your crown chakra of spirituality on the top

of your head. Imagine the light. Create it with the unlimited power of your mind. This is the Universal light of life energy, and you feel it stimulating this chakra center, which is purple in color. Visualize a swirling vortex of purple, and the light opens, balances, and charges this chakra center. Imagine the opening, balancing, charging.

(Pause for five seconds.)

And the light is now moving on down into the center of your forehead—your brow chakra, which is a swirling blue-violet vortex of energy. Perceive the blue-violet color, and feel the balancing and energizing that is taking place here.

Opening, balancing, energizing.

(Pause for five seconds.)

And the light is now moving on down into your throat chakra, which is a swirling silvery-blue vortex of energy.

Perceive the silvery-blue color, and feel the balancing and energizing that is taking place here. Opening, balancing, energizing.

(Pause for five seconds.)

And the light is now moving on down into your heart chakra, which is to be perceived as a golden glow. Perceive the golden color, and feel the balancing and energizing of your heart chakra center. Opening, balancing, energizing.

(Pause for five seconds.)

And the light is now moving on down into your solar plexus chakra, located at the level of your navel. This chakra is to be visualized as several shades of red in color. Perceive the red colors, and imagine the balancing and energizing that is taking place here. Opening, balancing, energizing.

(Pause for five seconds.)

And the light is moving on down into your sacral or spleen chakra, which is located a little below your navel. This swirling vortex of energy is a rainbow of colors. Perceive the many colors and feel the balancing and energizing that is taking place here. Opening, balancing, energizing.

(Pause for five seconds.)

And the light is now moving on down into your root chakra, at the base of your spine. This chakra is to be visualized as a swirling vortex of energy, red and orange in color. Perceive the reds and oranges, and feel the balancing and energizing that is taking place here. Opening, balancing, energizing.

(Pause for five seconds.)

And your chakras are opened, balanced, and charged, thus expanding your aura and attuning you to the subtle vibrations that support the perception of subjective awareness.

As you continue to focus upon the sound of my voice, I am going to count you down, down, down . . . so vividly imagine yourself in a situation going down . . . walking down stairs, downhill, down the side of a pyramid . . . or any situation in which you see yourself going down, while I count backwards from seven to one.

Number seven, deeper, deeper, deeper, down, down, down.

Number six, deeper, deeper, deeper, down, down, down.

Number five, deeper, deeper, deeper, down, down, down.

Number four, deeper, deeper, deeper, down, down, down.

Number three, deeper, deeper, deeper, down, down, down.

Number two, deeper, deeper, deeper, down, down, down.

Number one, deeper, deeper, deeper, down, down, down.

And you're relaxed and at ease and you feel deep. But let's go down a little deeper now . . . deeper now.

Number seven, deeper, deeper, deeper, down, down, down.

Number six, deeper, deeper, deeper, down, down, down.

Number five, deeper, deeper, deeper, down, down, down.

Number four, deeper, deeper, deeper, down, down, down.

Number three, deeper, deeper, deeper, down, down, down.

Number two, deeper, deeper, deeper, down, down, down.

Number one, deeper, deeper, deeper, down, down, down.

And you are now completely relaxed and at ease, and a quietness of spirit is filling your body and mind as you begin to focus upon your breathing . . . color breathing . . . deep, rhythmic, color breathing . . . as you begin to imagine a beautiful ball of swirling pale orchid energy . . . see it in your mind. The vibrant essence of this color. And perceive yourself merging with the color as you breathe deeply and relax completely. Pale orchid energy is surrounding you and filling you to overflowing with its vibrant essence.

Merge with the color and breathe it in . . . soothing pale orchid vibration, which causes you to relax even more . . . even more . . . breathing in the pale orchid vibration, and as you do, you feel yourself transcending the manifest world and opening to Higher Mind. Breathe in the color. Feel its vibration. Feel the inner harmony generated by the color . . . soothing your soul . . . soothing your soul . . . and when you need to relax and become harmonious, you will simply close your eyes and imagine this pale orchid color . . . and in so doing, you will begin to feel yourself let go of the physical and open to Higher Mind.

So go ahead and vividly imagine the pale orchid color . . . breathe in the vibration and experience the calming.

(Pause for forty-five seconds.)

And the pale orchid color is now beginning to change . . . to become a more intense violet. See it. Experience the change. Create the violet color with the unlimited power of your mind . . . a deeper and deeper shade of violet . . . a glowing violet that generates inner peace and protection . . . loving protection . . . security . . . serenity.

And whenever you choose to meditate upon the intense violet, you will experience a sense of inner peace . . . a feeling that all is well and everything will manifest for the greater good. Peaceful protection. Breathe in the soothing vibrations of the color. So go ahead and vividly imagine the violet color . . . breathe in the vibration and experience the feeling of peace and security.

(Pause for forty-five seconds.)

And you're relaxed and at ease and flowing with the music. And you now begin to perceive a bright green color off in the distance. See the green. Way off in the distance . . . and as you focus upon the green, you are transcending time and space . . . moving toward a grove of trees that are swaying in the breeze . . . and as you get closer and closer, you find that you can smell the scent of the outdoors after a light spring shower.

So refreshing . . . and as you float above the trees, you see a meadow . . . so go ahead and move to the meadow. Move to the meadow . . . float on down and land in the meadow . . . and perceive all the details.

It is so peaceful and serene, you want to sit down in the grass, so go ahead . . . feel the softness of the earth beneath you, Sit in the grass and breathe in the essence of nature . . . the calming green essence of nature . . . and as you do, look up in the sky and see a beautiful rainbow . . . a beautiful rainbow . . . perceive the different colors and intensity of the light and energy. Do this now while I'm quiet for a few moments.

(Pause for forty-five seconds.)

And as you observe the rainbow, know that the light and colors are wavelengths of energy, which can affect living tissue. Breathing in the appropriate color can effect a positive or healthful change in your body.

Continue to explore the colors of the rainbow: emerald green, turquoise blue, deep violet, rosy pink, radiant red, warm orange, and a golden hue. See how the colors meld into each other and yet how intense and separate they all seem to be.

(Pause for forty-five seconds.)

And as you continue to perceive the rainbow, consider your greatest need of healing. Maybe you need to become more positive, accepting, and compassionate. Maybe you need to soothe your soul and accept unalterable circumstances. Maybe you need physical healing or a return to vitality. If you don't consciously know which area is in most need of healing, allow your Higher Mind to do this for you.

Mentally focus on the area in need of healing as you observe the rainbow and allow the color that will be of most value to be drawn to you. Allow this to happen. Draw in the proper color ray to rejuvenate your body and mind. And perceive the color that is being drawn down to you. Breathe it in. Breathe in the color . . . and hold it as long as you comfortably can. Feel your body being filled to overflowing with the color . . . you are filled with and surrounded by the color. Breathe it in. Be with the experience as the color stimulates the portion of your body in most need of healing.

Breathe in the color. Become the color. Experience the healing. Do this while I'm quiet for a while.

(Pause for two minutes.)

You are healing. You are healed. And at any time you desire to do so, you can focus upon the color of most value to heal your body and mind.

And now it's time to create a mental movie in which you perceive yourself exactly as you desire to be. Your subconscious mind is a visual consciousness, so the most powerful programming is visual. By creating vivid images of who and what you desire to be, you literally create reality. So if it's healing you desire, create a mental movie in which you are healed. You are elated.

Those close to you are happy for you. Tap into your emotional response and the responses of others. See yourself being able to do what you desire to do, feel what you want to feel. OK, now you're the writer, director, producer, and star. So go ahead and vividly visualize while I'm quiet for a while.

(Pause for ninety seconds.)

And you've just seen your own reality. The images now become your reality. You now evoke the power of color healing, and it works for you. Every day in every way your condition improves. You are healing, you are healed. And every day in every way, you come closer to being all you can be.

And now it's time to return to the waking world.

And in just a moment I'm going to wake you up. On the count of five, you will open your eyes and be wide awake, fully alert, thinking and acting with calm self-assurance. You'll awaken feeling as if you've just taken a relaxing nap, and you'll be at peace with yourself, the world, and everyone in it.

Number one, coming on up now and feeling an expanding spiritual light within.

Number two, coming up feeling at peace with all life.

Number three, coming on up and tapping into an internal balance and harmony.

Number four, recall the situation in the room.

And number five, wide awake, wide awake. Open your eyes and feel good. Number five, wide awake.

Cord Cutting

Cord cutting is one of the most effective techniques for freeing someone you care about from a mind-fogging spell cast by dark entities.

A typical situation: You care very much about Rick, and you can plainly see that Nancy is taking advantage of him. When you discuss the situation with Rick, he becomes defensive and makes excuses for Nancy's actions. At the same time Rick is obviously frustrated with Nancy for constantly asking him to lend her money, which is never repaid, and for flirting with attractive men in his presence.

Describe the process: "Rick, Cord cutting is symbolic and real at the same time. There are branches or cords connecting the two of you: the longer you are together, the denser the connection. So in time, the branches become like a veil, blocking you from seeing what is really going on. But I can cut the cords so you can clearly see what Nancy's actions are generating.

"The branches or cords are invisible to our eyes, but if you could see the esoteric picture, you look like a huge bush. Some of the primary branches connecting you and Nancy are huge. She uses them to communicate with you and to program you. You could use them to do the same with her, but obviously it is not in your nature, and you have never tried.

"Sit in a chair or on the floor and close your eyes. I will begin to cut the cords between you and Nancy."

Snap a pair of imaginary scissors as you begin cutting the cords about four inches from the body, starting with his crown chakra on the top of his head. You can say any affirmation that suits the situation.

"Cutting the ties (clip, clip, clip). Clipping away the connection between Rick and Nancy once and for all. Go in peace, and leave Rick free. All attempts to control will backfire on thee.

"Cutting the ties (clip, clip, clip) between Rick and Nancy . . . go in peace, Nancy, and leave Rick free.

"By the dark and the light, your control ends tonight.

"Clipping away all connections."

Daily Healing Meditation

You're breathing deeply and relaxing completely. Breathing deeply and relaxing completely . . . and allowing a quietness of spirit to come in. Taking a deep breath in and holding it as long as you comfortably can . . . then let the breath out slowly through slightly parted lips, and when the breath is all the way out, push it further out, and further out . . . and then repeat the process. Breathing deeply, and when any outside thoughts come into your mind, simply brush them aside, tell yourself, "I'll deal with that later," and then return your concentration to the sound of my voice, and breathing deeply and relaxing completely.

And in just a moment I'm going to relax your body one part at a time. So play the role, play the part, and feel your body relaxing as I ask you to do so. And the relaxing power is coming into the toes of both of your feet at the same time . . . and it's moving right on down into the balls of your feet, into your arches, into your heels, and right on up to your ankles. Completely relaxed, completely relaxed . . . and the relaxing sensation now moves on up your legs to your knees, relaxing all the muscles as it goes. On up to your legs now, to your thighs and to your hips. Permeating every cell and every atom.

And you're relaxing completely, relaxing completely, keeping your full attention on the sound of my voice and relaxing your body, as the relaxing sensations move on down into the fingers of both of your hands . . . relaxing your hands. Feel your hands relaxing. And your lower arms are relaxed, and your upper arms are relaxed. Fingers and hands and lower arms and upper arms . . . just completely relaxed.

And the relaxing sensations now move on down into the base of your spine, your root chakra. Imagine a warmth in your root chakra as if a ray of sunlight were coming into the room and falling upon your spine . . . and it feels good. You imagine this warmth now moving up your spine . . . up your spine . . . up your spine and into the back of your neck and shoulder muscles. And your shoulder muscles are now loose and limp . . . loose and limp . . . just completely relaxed. And the relaxing sensations now move on up the back of your neck and into your scalp. Relaxing your scalp. Feel your scalp relaxing, and feel the relaxing sensations now drain down into your facial muscles, relaxing your facial muscles. Your jaw is relaxed. Allow a little space between your teeth. And your throat is relaxed. Your entire body is now relaxed all over in every way. And all tension is gone from your body and mind.

We're now going to balance and energize your aura and attune you to the subtle vibrations that support the perception of subjective awareness. So to begin, imagine a beam of iridescent white light coming down from above and entering your crown chakra of spirituality on the top of your head. Imagine the light . . . create it with the unlimited power of your mind. This is the Universal light of life energy, and you feel it stimulating this chakra center, which is purple in color. Visualize a swirling vortex of purple, and the light opens, balances, and charges this chakra center. Imagine the opening, balancing, charging.

(Pause for five seconds.)

And the light is now moving on down into the center of your forehead—your brow chakra, which is a swirling blue-violet vortex of energy. Perceive the blue-violet color, and feel the balancing and energizing that is taking place here.

Opening, balancing, energizing.

(Pause for five seconds.)

And the light is now moving on down into your throat chakra, which is a swirling silvery-blue vortex of energy.

Perceive the silvery-blue color, and feel the balancing and energizing that is taking place here. Opening, balancing, energizing.

(Pause for five seconds.)

And the light is now moving on down into your heart chakra, which is to be perceived as a golden glow. Perceive the golden color, and feel the balancing and energizing of your heart chakra center. Opening, balancing, energizing.

(Pause for five seconds.)

And the light is now moving on down into your solar plexus chakra, located at the level of your navel. This chakra is to be visualized as several shades of red in color. Perceive the red colors, and imagine the balancing and energizing that is taking place here. Opening, balancing, energizing.

(Pause for five seconds.)

And the light is moving on down into your sacral or spleen chakra, which is located a little below your navel.

This swirling vortex of energy is a rainbow of colors. Perceive the many colors, and feel the balancing and energizing that is taking place here. Opening, balancing, energizing.

(Pause for five seconds.)

And the light is now moving on down into your root chakra at the base of your spine. This chakra is to be visualized as a swirling vortex of energy, red and orange in color. Perceive the reds and oranges, and feel the balancing and energizing that is taking place here. Opening, balancing, energizing.

(Pause for five seconds.)

And your chakras are opened, balanced, and charged, thus expanding your aura and attuning you to the subtle vibrations that support the perception of subjective awareness.

And it's now time to imagine the bright white light moving back up into heart area. Visualize your heart center overflowing with the Universal light of life energy.

And now imagine the light emerging from your heart center to surround your body in a protective aura of bright white God light.

And you are totally protected. Totally protected. Only your own Guides and Masters or highly evolved and loving entities who mean you well will be able to influence you in any way in this altered state of consciousness session.

And as you continue to focus upon the sound of my voice, I am going to count you down, down, down . . . so vividly imagine yourself in a situation going down . . . walking down stairs, downhill, down the side of a pyramid . . .

or any situation in which you see yourself going down, while I count backwards from seven to one.

Number seven, deeper, deeper, deeper, down, down, down.

Number six, deeper, deeper, deeper, down, down, down.

Number five, deeper, deeper, deeper, down, down, down.

Number four, deeper, deeper, deeper, down, down, down.

Number three, deeper, deeper, deeper, down, down, down.

Number two, deeper, deeper, deeper, down, down, down.

Number one, deeper, deeper, deeper, down, down, down.

And you're relaxed and at ease and you feel deep. But let's go down a little deeper now ... deeper now.

Number seven, deeper, deeper, deeper, down, down, down.

Number six, deeper, deeper, deeper, down, down, down.

Number five, deeper, deeper, deeper, down, down, down.

Number four, deeper, deeper, deeper, down, down, down.

Number three, deeper, deeper, deeper, down, down, down.

Number two, deeper, deeper, deeper, down, down, down. Number one, deeper, deeper, deeper, down, down, down.

And you're now relaxed and at ease. A quietness of spirit fills your body and mind, and we're going to work together on healing. And we'll begin with positive suggestions, which will be communicated to every level of your body and mind. You are open to these suggestions and will accept and act upon them.

Your mind is all powerful and you now focus this power upon healing.

You now heal your body.

You consciously and subconsciously choose perfect health.

Every breath you take contains healing pranic energy.

Every cell in your body is filled with Divine healing light.

You are healing.

You are healed.

From this moment on, you think positive about your health.

Your body is rebuilding itself.

Every day, in every way, you get healthier.

You accept this. You are healing, you are healed.

And these suggestions have been communicated to every level of your body and mind, and they've been accepted on every level of your body and mind.

And your etheric body always maintains its original perfection. And you can use your perfect etheric body as a model for healing! So trust yourself and visualize your etheric body extending outside of your physical body . . . and your etheric body is eternally PERFECT.

Now imagine yourself in your prime of mental and physical health, and then perceive this shimmering image of your etheric body, which extends outside your physical body.

And now imagine that within you is the power to reproduce this etheric model within your physical body. Use the etheric as your model of perfection, replacing everything that is imperfect in your physical form. You can do this. Use the unlimited power of your mind to replicate your etheric body within your physical body. Do it. Be healed. Vividly imagine the process.

(Pause for thirty seconds.)

And now, to increase the power with which you can align your etheric and physical bodies, let's do an exercise to unblock your natural healing flow, which is abundant. So now imagine the light coming down from above once again, only this time it's a blue light . . . an intense, shimmering, iridescent blue light coming down from above . . . entering your crown chakra of spirituality . . . and it begins to flow through your body and mind . . . through your entire body . . . and as it does, it unblocks your natural healing flow. Feel it! Feel it! Allow the light to heal you. Mentally match your physical body to your etheric body.

(Pause for sixty seconds.)

And the more you incorporate love and compassion and positive thoughts into your life, the more you raise your vibrational rate, which assists the healing process.

And it's time to invoke the power of a mantra to communicate your wishes to every level of your body and mind, so say the words along with me, silently in your mind: "Using my perfect etheric body as a model, I now reproduce this perfection in my physical form." (Say this ten times.)

That's right . . . using your perfect etheric body as a model, you now reproduce this perfection in your physical form, which generates healing. And you are healing, you are healed.

And in just a moment I'm going to wake you up. On the count of five, you will open your eyes and be wide awake, fully alert, thinking and acting with calm self-assurance. You'll awaken feeling as if you've just taken a relaxing nap, and you'll be at peace with yourself, the world, and everyone in it.

Number one, coming on up now and feeling an expanding spiritual light within.

Number two, coming up feeling at peace with all life.

Number three, coming on up and tapping into an internal balance and harmony.

Number four, recall the situation in the room.

And number five, wide awake, wide awake. Open your eyes and feel good. Number five, wide awake.

Desires and Possibilities

What you desire you also fear. You can choose to experience the fear or avoid it. Avoidance will be safer but may offer less growth potential. Karmically, neither choice is right or wrong. Your decision generates an opportunity, and the outcome will provide the lessons.

What you resist you draw to you. You've all heard that, but from a karmic perspective, that which you resist you become, unless you learn through love and wisdom.

The Desires Process

Take a moment to meditate upon something you desire and the fear that accompanies the desire, and think about the different ways you can respond to the desire: your potential choices.

If you're considering the pursuit of this desire, you're considering risk. Behind every risk is a fear of loss: the loss of love, loss of control, or loss of self-esteem. Which applies to your risk?

(Pause for ten seconds.)

What is the clear purpose of your desire?

(Pause for ten seconds.)

If you attempt to fulfill your desire, what is the best that could happen if things work out in your favor?

(Pause for ten seconds.)

What is the worst that could happen if it didn't work out? (Pause for ten seconds.)

Is the potential loss greater than the possible gain?

(Pause for ten seconds.)

Who else would like to see you fulfill your desire?

(Pause for ten seconds.)

If you're afraid in regard to pursuing your desire, what is holding you back?

(Pause for ten seconds.)

If you fulfill your desire, will it result in a more honest, freer life?

(Pause for ten seconds.)

Would your fulfilled desire be a growth step that could improve the quality of your life?

(Pause for ten seconds.)

You can't grow without taking chances. If you've decided to pursue your desire, don't sit back and wait for the perfect moment to act.

(Pause for ten seconds.)

If you are considering the pursuit of an emotional desire, realize the risk is simply being honest in expressing your feelings.

The Possibilities Process

Change begins with recognizing potentials and thinking about them in a positive way. While you do this process, vividly imagine with mental movies for the best results.

What is it you'd most like to do that you don't do?

(Pause for ten seconds.)

What would you do if you weren't worried about what other people might think? You'd be dropping a mask, wouldn't you?

(Pause for ten seconds.)

What if you were able to do anything you enjoy? To start, I'd like you to create a mental movie in which you imagine yourself giving up what you don't like doing. See yourself telling someone that you won't be doing this any-more. You're going to delegate the job to someone else. Then imagine how you'd spend the time that you've gained.

What about it? Go do it!

(Pause for two minutes.)

Five years into the future: you are happier and more successful than you ever dreamed possible. Exactly what are you doing?

(Pause for ten seconds.)

What are the circumstances you find yourself experiencing?

(Pause for ten seconds.)

This process represents *aliveness*. You become aware of how you think. If its not positive, your mind has the power and ability to change.

Earthbound Entity Attachment

It is absolutely necessary to talk about the subject before you do this process. Your client should have already met their Spirit Guide (see the chapter below, "Spirit Guides"), who has probably answered questions regarding the primary issues in their life. Resolve your client's anxiety, but don't let them know when you are going to check for entity attachments. It is advised that your subject is in deep hypnosis and in a Higher Self level.

Hypnotist: All right, (client), I'm going to ask a question of your Spirit Guide, (name of Spirit Guide). She will immediately answer yes or no, and she will project that reply into your mind. You'll hear it with your inner ears or as a strong thought, and you will perceive the answer and immediately speak up and share it with me.

OK, (Spirit Guide), you've been with (client) all his (or her) life. You know him (or her) on every level of body, mind, and spirit. And here's my question to you: is there an earthbound entity instead of (client's) body at this time . . . yes or no?

Spirit Guide: Yes.

Hypnotist: OK, thank you, (Spirit Guide). How many entities are residing in (client's) body? (Note: entities are nonphysical, and although they usually cannot leave a body once they're inside, they don't take up any room. The usual number would be between one and five, but there could be hundreds or even thousands.)

Spirit Guide: Three.

Hypnotist: All right, (client). I need to directly communicate with the entities, so I need you to momentarily allow the entities to use your vocal cords to communicate with me.

Client: (nods yes).

Hypnotist: (Speaking louder and more forcefully) OK, I'm speaking directly to the entities in (client's) body. I know that one of you has assumed the role of leader or the one who presumes to speak for the others. So I need to talk to you right now. Please speak up and communicate with me.

(If the entity doesn't speak up within thirty seconds): I'm waiting. If you don't speak up, I will have to have you immediately removed from John's body. So please communicate with me now.

Entity: We don't need you!

(The entity may speak in a normal voice, or they may growl out their response and even become threatening. As the hypnotist, you must remain calm and in control.)

Hypnotist: I'm sure you don't think you need me, but I can have you removed, so it's best you talk with me. What is your name?

Entity: (Gives name.)

Hypnotist: Can you speak for the others in (client's) body, (entity)?

Entity: Yes.

Hypnotist: How long have you been residing in (client's) body?

Entity: Since he visited the hospital.

Note: Once the entity is directly communicating with you, keep the conversation going for a while by asking questions such as, "I realize you probably died in the hospital, but why was (client's) body open to you?" The entity will say something like, "He was very depressed when his mother died."

"How long ago did you die, (entity)?" "How did you die?" "Did the other's residing in (client's) body join you before or after your arrival?" "What were the circumstances when (name of other entity) joined you?" You can spend about ten minutes talking with whoever is willing to speak up.

Now it's time to start talking about the entity leaving. For example: "Well, you know, (entity), when (client) looks in the mirror, you also see the reflection, and (client's) body certainly isn't your body. You do realize that, don't you? If you go to the Light, you'll be able to begin again, having your own body once again. Within the Light are all the tools of manifestation, (entity)."

If the entity is unwilling or scared to leave, you can make one of two choices, usually depending upon how much time you have.

1. Bring in someone the entity knew and loved in life. Usually their mother, or their mate, or a close friend who has crossed over. Ask whoever comes in to explain what will happen if the entity goes with this person into the Light. Then you remain quiet for a while. In a couple of minutes, ask the entities if they are willing to be guided into the light.

2. I call in Archangel Michael, who always comes. Explain to Michael that the entities don't want to leave, and they are harming John, so vacating his body is important. Ask Michael to explain what will happen if the entities follow him into the light. Give Michael time for this. Then ask that they be removed. When this is done, thank Michael for his assistance.

Hypnotist: (Client,) you'll feel Archangel Michael's light surrounding your body with love and protection. And now focus once again upon the God light coming down from above and entering your crown chakra of spirituality on the top of your head. The light is moving through your chakra system . . . down . . . into your heart area, where it is beginning to concentrate. Every cell and every atom is permeated with this God light . . . This healing ray of bright white God light, feel it, see it with your inner eyes. Your heart area is filled with the God light. Every cell and every atom, filled to overflowing with this shimmering, iridescent God light.

This healing ray of bright white God light, feel it, see it with your inner eyes. Your heart area is filled with the God light. Every cell and every atom, filled to overflowing with the shimmering, iridescent God light.

Sense the light concentrating around your heart area, filling you to overflowing. See and sense the light . . .

(One minute of these kinds of suggestions, or silence.)

And now, release the light from your heart area, allowing it to totally surround your body in a protectory aura of shimmering God light. You are totally surrounded in an aura of God light. See it in your mind. Feel it. Sense it. You are totally surrounded, sealed in this God light. And from this moment, you are protected from all things, seen and unseen, all forces and all elements. Only your own Guides or loving entities who mean you well will be able to influence you in any way. And you are sealed in the God light. We ask in thy divine name, we beseech it, we mark it . . . and so it is.

Then go on to provide your client with additional suggestions before awakening them.

Ending note: It is advised that you always make a mind-programming audio recording with major sessions. When the induction is complete, as the first suggestion, it is wise to seal the client's body in the God light. Then, every time they listen to the audio, the sealing is reinforced.

Four Relationship Killers

Close your eyes and do a few minutes of deep breathing.

Now think about a time you were upset by a lover in a past or present relationship ... OK, now think about another time you were upset, and another time ...

All right, can you get that in each case, you were upset because you didn't get what you wanted? *In other words, you weren't in control of your lover. It all boils down to control.* Maybe you wanted your lover's approval and didn't get it. Maybe you wanted your lover to be the way you wanted your lover to be, and it didn't happen. Maybe you wanted more respect or consideration, or for your lover to be more responsible, or passionate, or monogamous ... But you didn't get what you wanted, and you got upset. You wanted to control your lover, and you didn't get your way. Most of the conflicts in our lives are the result of our trying to control situations.

In love, we don't want to feel pain, so we try to control our relationship. We try to avoid rejection, loss, and jealousy by controlling our lover. But the need to control is a FEAR-BASED EMOTION, and it never works. Usually it just pushes the other person away.

All right, the first relationship killer is CRITICISM of your lover ... I'd like you to recall a time that you expressed criticism and then realize that you were trying to control your lover through criticism.

(Pause for one minute.)

OK, the second relationship killer is CONTEMPT for your lover . . . Recall a time you expressed contempt, and then realize that in expressing contempt, you were trying to control your lover through this expression of disapproval.

(Pause for one minute.)

All right, the third relationship killer is BEING DEFEN-SIVE . . . Recall a time you were defensive with your lover, and realize that in being defensive, you were trying to control your lover through your response.

(Pause for one minute.)

OK, the fourth relationship killer is WITHDRAWAL . . . Recall a time you withdrew from your lover, and realize that in withdrawing, you were trying to control your lover through your actions.

(Pause for one minute.)

All right, let go of this. And realize that control is FEAR. And if fear is the problem, LOVE is the answer . . . and twin-flame or counterpart soul mate love is unconditional love.

Evolved soul mate love is an expression of self-actualization in which you accept others without judgment, or blame, or expectations. Self-actualized soul mate love rises above the need to control and the four relationship killers of criticism, contempt, defensiveness, and with-drawal.

Open your eyes.

"If Only"

All too often, we look for solutions externally. We think, "If only I could find my soul mate, life would really work. If only I made more money, I'd be happy. If only my lover gave me more sex (or maybe less sex), I wouldn't be frustrated. If only I could sell my novel, my career would take off. If only I could lose some weight, I'd feel better about myself. If only my mother-in-law stayed out of my life, I wouldn't be so frustrated. If only I had a brain, I could function better."

"If onlys" begin externally; then, as we resolve them, we eventually begin to look inside. New Agers are different from others. If they get past thinking their soul mate, more money, or self-discipline will provide them with satisfaction, they think spiritual awareness will do it: "If only I could attain enlightenment, I'd be peaceful. If only I were psychic, I would know my life purpose, and everything would work."

But even if you got these things, they wouldn't change much for very long. The right relationship can't make you feel better about yourself. More money won't generate happiness. All the "if onlys" will simply generate more "if onlys." More of the same. More of whatever is going on in your life that isn't working.

There was a man whose "if only" was about not having enough money. Then he started his own business, and now he is doing very well. He has an abundance of money, and his "if only" is about having enough free time to enjoy the money. He says his career is consuming his life. But if he had the money and the time, his "if only" would be, "If only I had a loving relationship, I could enjoy what I have."

We all have an "I want" viewpoint. It's all about "ME . . . MY NEEDS." That's just what is. Just the way it works as human beings.

We try to avoid pain and get what we want.

The result is anxiety—unease. And in response to our anxiety, we find "avoids." Places to hide, such as overeating, drinking or drugs, overworking, watching TV to excess. We hide out in these places to repress our anxiety. Over the years, it gets worse and worse as we buy into our "if onlys."

Nothing is going to change in your life unless you wake up and get off it. We need to rise above the fear. *Enlightenment is an absence—an absence of fear.*

Enlightenment is an absence of "if onlys" . . . an absence of the "I wants" . . . an absence of all the fear-based emotions, such as possessiveness, jealousy, hate, greed, guilt, envy, insecurity, blame, resentment, repression, judgment, and prejudice. Enlightenment is also about accepting other people without judgment, blame, or expectations.

Human-potential trainers sometimes get discouraged because they don't see change in people close to them. They have the understanding, but nothing changes. Sometimes trainers don't see change in themselves. And that's *really* bothersome.

It's nice to think we can learn to let go of things, get rid of things. But experience often says that doesn't really work. We don't let go of *anything*. It sounds good, and some people claim to be able to do it, but in reality, it just isn't something many of us can do.

Instead, we seem to wear things out. We get obsessed with our issues, or a person, or an idea, or a desire . . . and we play our obsession, and play it, and play it, until we wear it out . . . or we act on it . . . or we make ourselves crazy.

The more you obsess, the faster you burn through your obsession, or the sooner you act upon it. But keep in mind that you are not your thoughts. Let your thoughts play out in your mind, and observe them like a TV show. You'll come to realize that 90 percent of your thoughts are unreal. Wasted energy. Useless opinions, memories, judgments, desires, and manipulations to try to get what you want. They fill your head with unreality, and they can waste your life.

There is nothing wrong with fantasizing, but do not accept your fantasies as reality. Observe them for what they are.

They're part of what it means to be a human being—part of living with other people. The idea is to *wake up* to reality.

The "If Only" Process

You're breathing deeply and relaxing completely. Breathing deeply and relaxing completely . . . and allowing a quietness of spirit to come in. Taking a deep breath in and holding it as long as you comfortably can ... then let the breath out slowly through slightly parted lips, and when the breath is all the way out, push it further out, and further out ... and then repeat the process. Breathing deeply, and when any outside thoughts come into your mind, simply brush them aside and tell yourself, "I'll deal with that later," and then return your concentration to the sound of my voice, and breathing deeply and relaxing completely.

And in just a moment I'm going to relax your body one part at a time. So play the role, play the part, and feel your body relaxing as I ask you to do so. And the relaxing power is coming into the toes of both of your feet at the same time ... and it's moving right on down into the balls of your feet, into your arches, into your heels, and right on up to your ankles. Completely relaxed, completely relaxed ... and the relaxing sensations now move on up your legs to your knees, relaxing all the muscles as it goes. And on up your legs now, to your thighs and to your hips. Permeating every cell and every atom.

And you're relaxing completely, relaxing completely, keeping your full attention on the sound of my voice and relaxing your body, as the relaxing sensations move on down into the fingers of both of your hands ... relaxing your hands. Feel your hands relaxing. And your lower arms are relaxed, and your upper arms are relaxed. Fingers and hands and lower arms and upper arms ... just completely relaxed.

And the relaxing sensations now move on down into the base of your spine, your root chakra. Imagine a warmth in your root chakra as if a ray of sunlight were coming into the room and falling upon your spine ... and it feels good.

You imagine this warmth now moving up your spine . . . up your spine . . . up your spine and into the back of your neck and shoulder muscles. And your shoulder muscles are now loose and limp . . . loose and limp . . . just completely relaxed. And the relaxing sensations now move on up the back of your neck and into your scalp. Relaxing your scalp. Feel your scalp relaxing, and feel the relaxing sensations now drain down into your facial muscles, relaxing your facial muscles. Your jaw is relaxed. Allow a little space between your teeth. And your throat is relaxed. Your entire body is now relaxed all over in every way. And all tension is gone from your body and mind.

And as you continue to focus upon the sound of my voice, I am going to count you down, down, down . . . so vividly imagine yourself in a situation going down . . . walking down stairs, downhill, down the side of a pyramid . . . or any situation in which you see yourself going down, while I count backwards from seven to one.

Number seven, deeper, deeper, deeper, down, down, down.

Number six, deeper, deeper, deeper, down, down, down.

Number five, deeper, deeper, deeper, down, down, down.

Number four, deeper, deeper, deeper, down, down, down.

Number three, deeper, deeper, deeper, down, down, down.

Number two, deeper, deeper, deeper, down, down, down. Number one, deeper, deeper, deeper, down, down, down.

And you're relaxed and at ease, and you feel deep. But let's go down a little deeper now . . . deeper now.

Number seven, deeper, deeper, deeper, down, down, down.

Number six, deeper, deeper, deeper, down, down, down.

Number five, deeper, deeper, deeper, down, down, down.

Number four, deeper, deeper, deeper, down, down, down.

Number three, deeper, deeper, deeper, down, down, down.

Number two, deeper, deeper, deeper, down, down, down. Number one, deeper, deeper, deeper, down, down, down.

And you are now completely relaxed and at ease. And if you feel uncomfortable at any time, you can easily bring yourself up by counting up from one to five and saying the words, "Wide awake."

All right, now trust the first thoughts the come into your mind in response to each of my directives.

Explore your relationship "if onlys."

(Pause for sixty seconds.)

Explore your "if onlys" with friends.

(Pause for sixty seconds.)

Explore your "if onlys" in regard to what you really want out of life.

(Pause for sixty seconds.)

What are your "if onlys" about your job?

(Pause for sixty seconds.)

Do you have any career-level "if onlys?"

(Pause for sixty seconds.)

Examine all your "if onlys," and pick your primary one. Your primary "if only."

(Pause for sixty seconds.)

How many of your "if onlys" require someone else to be the way you want them to be?

(Pause for sixty seconds.)

Imagine yourself just observing your "if onlys." Not buying into them. Not responding to them. Just observing . . . detached.

And in just a moment I'm going to wake you up. On the count of five, you will open your eyes and be wide awake, fully alert, thinking and acting with calm self-assurance. You'll awaken feeling as if you've just taken a relaxing nap, and you'll be at peace with yourself, the world, and everyone in it.

Number one, coming on up now and feeling an expanding spiritual light within.

Number two, coming up feeling at peace with all life.

Number three, coming on up and tapping into an internal balance and harmony.

Number four, recall the situation in the room.

And number five, wide awake, wide awake. Open your eyes and feel good. Number five, wide awake.

Intuitive Writing

You're breathing deeply and relaxing completely.

Breathing deeply and relaxing completely . . . and allowing a quietness of spirit to come in. Taking a deep breath in and holding it as long as you comfortably can . . . then let the breath out slowly through slightly parted lips, and when the breath is all the way out, push it further out, and further out . . . and then repeat the process. Breathing deeply, and when any outside thoughts come into your mind, simply brush them aside and tell yourself, "I'll deal with that later," and then return your concentration to the sound of my voice, and breathing deeply and relaxing completely.

And in just a moment I'm going to relax your body one part at a time. So play the role, play the part, and feel your body relaxing as I ask you to do so. And the relaxing power is coming into the toes of both of your feet at the same time . . . and it's moving right on down into the balls of your feet, into your arches, into your heels, and right on up to your ankles. Completely relaxed, completely relaxed . . . and the relaxing sensations now move on up your legs to your knees, relaxing all the muscles as they go. And on up your legs now, to your thighs and to your hips. Permeating every cell and every atom.

And you're relaxing completely, relaxing completely, keeping your full attention on the sound of my voice and relaxing your body, as the relaxing sensations move on down into the fingers of both of your hands . . . relaxing your hands. Feel your hands relaxing. And your lower arms are relaxed, and your upper arms are relaxed. Fingers and hands and lower arms and upper arms . . . just completely relaxed.

And the relaxing sensations now move on down into the base of your spine, your root chakra. Imagine a warmth in your root chakra as if a ray of sunlight were coming into the room and falling upon your spine . . . and it feels good. You imagine this warmth now moving up your spine . . . up your spine . . . up your spine and into the back of your neck and shoulder muscles. And your shoulder muscles are now loose and limp . . . loose and limp . . . just completely relaxed. And the relaxing sensations now move on up the back of your neck and into your scalp. Relaxing your scalp. Feel your scalp relaxing, and feel the relaxing sensations now drain down into your facial muscles, relaxing your facial muscles. Your jaw is relaxed. Allow a little space between your teeth. And your throat is relaxed. Your entire body is now relaxed all over in every way. And all tension is gone from your body and mind.

We're now going to balance and energize your aura and attune you to the subtle vibrations that support the perception of subjective awareness. So to begin, imagine a beam of iridescent white light coming down from above and entering your crown chakra of spirituality on the top of your head. Imagine the light . . . create it with the unlimited power of your mind. This is the Universal light of life energy, and you feel it stimulating this chakra center, which is purple in color. Visualize a swirling vortex of purple, and the light opens, balances, and charges this chakra center. Imagine the opening, balancing, charging.

(Pause for five seconds.)

And the light is now moving on down into the center of your forehead—your brow chakra, which is a swirling blue-violet vortex of energy. Perceive the blue-violet color, and feel the balancing and energizing that is taking place here.

Opening, balancing, energizing.

(Pause for five seconds.)

And the light is now moving on down into your throat chakra, which is a swirling silvery-blue vortex of energy.

Perceive the silvery-blue color, and feel the balancing and energizing that is taking place here. Opening, balancing, energizing.

(Pause for five seconds.)

And the light is now moving on down into your heart chakra, which is to be perceived as a golden glow. Perceive the golden color, and feel the balancing and energizing of your heart chakra center. Opening, balancing, energizing.

(Pause for five seconds.)

And the light is now moving on down into your solar plexus chakra, located at the level of your navel. This chakra is to be visualized as several shades of red in color. Perceive the red colors, and imagine the balancing and energizing that is taking place here. Opening, balancing, energizing.

(Pause for five seconds.)

And the light is moving on down into your sacral or spleen chakra, which is located a little below your navel. This swirling vortex of energy is a rainbow of colors. Perceive the many colors and feel the balancing and energizing that is taking place here. Opening, balancing, energizing.

(Pause for five seconds.)

And the light is now moving on down into your root chakra at the base of your spine. This chakra is to be visualized as a swirling vortex of energy, red and orange in color. Perceive the reds and oranges, and feel the balancing and energizing that is taking place here. Opening, balancing, energizing.

(Pause for five seconds.)

And your chakras are opened, balanced, and charged, thus expanding your aura and attuning you to the subtle vibrations that support the perception of subjective awareness.

And it's now time to imagine the bright white light moving back up into heart area. Visualize your heart center overflowing with the Universal light of life energy.

And now imagine the light emerging from your heart center to surround your body in a protective aura of bright white God light.

And you are totally protected. Totally protected. Only your own Guides and Masters or highly evolved and loving entities who mean you well will be able to influence you in any way in this altered state of consciousness session.

As you continue to focus upon the sound of my voice, I am going to count you down, down, down ... so vividly imagine yourself in a situation going down ... walking down stairs, downhill, down the side of a pyramid ... or any situation in which you see yourself going down, while I count backwards from seven to one.

Number seven, deeper, deeper, deeper, down, down, down.

Number six, deeper, deeper, deeper, down, down, down.

Number five, deeper, deeper, deeper, down, down, down.

Number four, deeper, deeper, deeper, down, down, down.

Number three, deeper, deeper, deeper, down, down, down.

Number two, deeper, deeper, deeper, down, down, down. Number one, deeper, deeper, deeper, down, down, down.

And you're relaxed and at ease, and you feel deep. But let's go down a little deeper now ... deeper now.

Number seven, deeper, deeper, deeper, down, down, down.

Number six, deeper, deeper, deeper, down, down, down.

Number five, deeper, deeper, deeper, down, down, down.

Number four, deeper, deeper, deeper, down, down, down.

Number three, deeper, deeper, deeper, down, down, down.

Number two, deeper, deeper, deeper, down, down, down. Number one, deeper, deeper, deeper, down, down, down.

And you're now relaxed and at ease and peacefully centered, and you feel in balance and in harmony. A quietness of spirit permeates your body and mind, and we are now going to work together to open a channel for successful automatic writing.

You absolutely have the power and ability to step outside of yourself and allow the energy of your Higher Mind, or an entity of your choice, to communicate through your hand through automatic writing.

All right . . . it's time to call in your Guides and Masters to assist you and to spiritually protect you during this session. Call out silently in your mind. Call them in. Hear your voice echo out across the universe and back to you.

(Pause for sixty seconds.)

And now . . . focus upon what you desire to learn through automatic writing. Read the question you wrote down, silently in your mind . . . and now repeat it over and over as a mental mantra.

(Pause for sixty seconds.)

And it's time to make contact with the source of the information you are seeking. So do this now. Again, silently in your mind, make your wishes known. Call out to the entity or source you want to contact through intuitive and automatic writing. Ask them to join you, to open and write through your hand so you may attain information you desire to know.

(Pause for sixty seconds.)

And your Guides and Masters are right there with you. The source of awareness is at hand. And it's now time to intensify the spiritual protection, so visualize very, very vividly the white light coming down from above and entering, once again, into your crown chakra at the top of your head. Now visualize this beam of God light concentrating around you heart area, filling your heart chakra. And now, imagine the light emerging from your heart area and totally surrounding you in an aura of bright white, protective God light.

(Pause for ten seconds.)

And you seek divine protection in the white light of God's love. You seek protection from all things seen and unseen, all forces and all elements, protecting you and assuring only sincere contact with highly evolved and loving entities, or with your Higher mind. You ask it, you beseech it, you mark it . . . and so it is. And you are totally protected. Only your own Guides and Master or those you invite may influence you in any way or communicate through your hand.

(Pause for ten seconds.)

All right. In just a moment I will direct you to open your eyes and begin writing. You absolutely have the power and ability to allow the energy to flow through you and to receive awareness through this technique. When you open your eyes, they will be just barely open, and you will keep your pen moving at all times . . . and on the count of three, you will open your eyes and begin to write using your intuition automatically. Open to the awareness. Allow it to come through. Number one, number two, number three.

(Pause for fifteen to twenty minutes.)

All right. You now have just another minute to finish up.

(Pause for sixty seconds.)

And now take a moment to thank the source of your awareness, knowing that you can always return on your own to continue automatic writing.

(Pause for thirty seconds.)

And in just a moment I'm going to wake you up. On the count of five, you will open your eyes and be wide awake, fully alert, thinking and acting with calm self-assurance. You'll awaken feeling as if you've just taken a relaxing nap, and you'll be at peace with yourself, the world, and everyone in it.

Number one, coming on up now and feeling an expanding spiritual light within.

Number two, coming up feeling at peace with all life.

Number three, coming on up and tapping into an internal balance and harmony.

Number four, recall the situation in the room.

And number five, wide awake, wide awake. Open your eyes and feel good. Number five, wide awake.

Masks

Some newer forms of psychotherapy (Morita Therapy, Reality Therapy, Naikan Therapy) focus on changing your behavior: you don't have to change how you feel about something to affect it, as long as you're willing to change what you're doing.

Change begins with action. *Karma* means *action*, and wisdom erases karma.

The six blocks that keep you from acting:
1. Lack of clarity
2. Fear of change
3. Waiting for someone or something to step in and save you
4. Lack of aliveness or motivation
5. Overwhelm
6. Doubting your ability to accomplish the goal, and thus not acting

Action starts with finding out who you are behind your masks. Masks are deceptive words, deeds, and facial expressions you use to cast an image that is not really who you are. You wear masks to keep out fear, avoid loss, and get what you want. Masks are forms of repression, and repression is a problem we all share.

Repression doesn't go away. It simply lies deep within, waiting for an opportunity to express itself. From the perspective of long-term harm, repression is worse than indulgence, because you will eventually get tired of what you indulge in. Poet William Blake said, "The road to excess leads to the palace of wisdom."

Let's explore your masks, because you can't change what you don't recognize. You wear masks to hide who you really are. You probably don't even realize you're wearing them. But you're wearing a mask even when you smile when you don't really want to smile.

There are three reasons to explore your masks:

1. To learn why you wear them. The cause will always be a fear.
2. To learn the price of wearing a mask: it will generate stress of some kind.
3. To see if the mask is still valid. Often, when a mask is no longer needed, people continue to wear it out of habit.

When you're honest and direct, you don't need a mask. It takes no energy to be honest and direct, and there is no repression. The underlying philosophy behind self-actualized thinking is openness and honesty.

Even the need to seem like a good person is often a mask. You always act in your own self-interest all of the time. That may not be the way you want it to be, but it is what is. For many, believing they are selfless and altruistic is a way to hide from the fact that deep down inside, they don't feel important. In claiming to be selfless, they gain enormously in self-esteem. But this is nonsense.

You do what you do because in some way it serves you. If you devote yourself to taking care of your sick mother, you do it for *you*. Maybe you have a self-image of what a good son or daughter does, and if you were to turn away from your mother during her time of need, your self-image would be irreparably damaged. Maybe you run into a burning building to save a child, or into the ocean to save a stranger. For whatever reason, it was for you. Maybe you would not want to live knowing that you might have saved them and you were too cowardly to act. But you would do it for *you*, although others are served in the process. So it's not really sacrifice.

Some look to figures like Albert Schweitzer and Mahatma Gandhi as models of altruism. But when people talked to Schweitzer about his wonderful work, he told them he enjoyed doing what he did. It was no big deal. Gandhi set cause and effect into play and then continued to choose between the available alternatives as circumstances unfolded. He fulfilled his work and was served. And millions of others were served as well.

Nevertheless, martyrs and do-gooders are usually among the most selfish of people, for they have insatiable egos.

You can choose to be rationally or irrationally selfish. It is irrational selfishness that causes us to cringe. Rational selfishness is a matter of responding to the needs of others to obtain our own objectives. You need to give to receive in human relationships.

Everyone is selfish. It's like saying gravity exists. So what? That's what is. Yet people don't fight gravity. They do fight the idea of being selfish.

This does not mean to stop assisting your fellow human beings. It does mean to stop fooling yourself about *why* you assist them.

Stop being a martyr. Stop waiting for people to express gratitude. You did it for *you*. Stop waiting for your gold star.

These are the following four steps to end suffering and obtain peace of mind:

1. Accept karma as your philosophical basis of reality. In so doing, you accept self-responsibility.
2. Accept that "what is, is."
3. Develop detached mind.
4. Accept that viewpoint is the deciding factor in how you experience life.

The Masks Process

You're breathing deeply and relaxing completely.

Breathing deeply and relaxing completely . . . and allowing a quietness of spirit to come in. Taking a deep breath in and holding it as long as you comfortably can . . . then let the breath out slowly through slightly parted lips, and when the breath is all the way out, push it further out, and further out . . . and then repeat the process. Breathing deeply, and when any outside thoughts come into your mind, simply brush them aside and tell yourself, "I'll deal with that later," and then return your concentration to the sound of my voice, and breathing deeply and relaxing completely.

And in just a moment, I'm going to relax your body one part at a time. So play the role, play the part, and feel your body relaxing as I ask you to do so. And the relaxing power is coming into the toes of both of your feet at the same time . . . and it's moving right on down into the balls of your feet, into your arches, into your heels, and right on up to your ankles. Completely relaxed, completely relaxed . . . and the relaxing sensations now move on up your legs to your knees, relaxing all the muscles as it goes. And on up your legs now, to your thighs and to your hips. Permeating every cell and every atom.

And you're relaxing completely, relaxing completely, keeping your full attention on the sound of my voice and relaxing your body, as the relaxing sensations move on down into the fingers of both of your hands . . . relaxing your hands. Feel your hands relaxing. And your lower arms are relaxed, and your upper arms are relaxed. Fingers and hands and lower arms and upper arms . . . just completely relaxed.

And the relaxing sensations now move on down into the base of your spine, your root chakra. Imagine a warmth in your root chakra as if a ray of sunlight were coming into the room and falling upon your spine . . . and it feels good. You imagine this warmth now moving up your spine . . . up your spine . . . up your spine and into the back of your neck and shoulder muscles. And your shoulder muscles are now loose and limp . . . loose and limp . . . just completely relaxed. And the relaxing sensations now move on up the back of your neck and into your scalp. Relaxing your scalp. Feel your scalp relaxing, and feel the relaxing sensations now drain down into your facial muscles, relaxing your facial muscles. Your jaw is relaxed. Allow a little space between your teeth. And your throat is relaxed. Your entire body is now relaxed all over in every way. And all tension is gone from your body and mind.

As you continue to focus upon the sound of my voice, I am going to count you down, down, down . . . so vividly imagine yourself in a situation going down . . . walking down stairs, downhill, down the side of a pyramid . . . or in any situation in which you see yourself going down, while I count backwards from seven to one.

Number seven, deeper, deeper, deeper, down, down, down.

Number six, deeper, deeper, deeper, down, down, down.

Number five, deeper, deeper, deeper, down, down, down.

Number four, deeper, deeper, deeper, down, down, down.

Number three, deeper, deeper, deeper, down, down, down.

Number two, deeper, deeper, deeper, down, down, down.

Number one, deeper, deeper, deeper, down, down, down.

And you're relaxed and at ease and you feel deep. But let's go down a little deeper now . . . deeper now.

Number seven, deeper, deeper, deeper, down, down, down.

Number six, deeper, deeper, deeper, down, down, down.

Number five, deeper, deeper, deeper, down, down, down.

Number four, deeper, deeper, deeper, down, down, down. Number three, deeper, deeper, deeper, down, down, down.

Number two, deeper, deeper, deeper, down, down, down. Number one, deeper, deeper, deeper, down, down, down.

And you're now relaxed and at ease and centered upon achieving your goals. You are at peace and feel in balance and in harmony. A quietness of spirit permeates your body and mind . . . and you're open to awareness that will assist you to rise above repression and the fears in your life.

There are three ways to generate change in a human being. The first is to add something, such as people, things, environment, programming, trust, responsibility, awareness, and challenge. The second is to subtract something, such as people, things, environment, guilt, fear, trust, or loss of health. And third is to get the person to be who they really are . . . which is transcendental change. The individual removes fear pretenses, drops masks, and expands.

Even if you don't like what you find out, accepting what is in yourself is the beginning of transformation. You can always change what isn't working, but you can't change what you don't recognize.

Most of us don't even realize we're wearing masks that keep us from being who we really are. So let's begin to explore the masks you wear.

There are three primary reasons to examine yours. The first is to learn why you wear it. There will always be a fear behind the mask. The second reason is to become aware of the price you pay for wearing the mask. There will always be a price. And the third is to see if the reason you're wearing the mask is still valid. Often it isn't, but you continue to wear the mask out of habit.

So, let's begin by exploring what you consider to be your primary mask. When do you most repress who you really are? Is it that you don't do what you want to do? You don't say what you want to say? Take a few moments to think of your primary mask.

(Pause for forty seconds.)

All right, now behind every mask is a fear. What is the fear that keeps you from expressing who you really are?

(Pause for thirty seconds.)

And now, what is the price you pay for wearing this mask?

There's always a price. You either take out your repressed emotions on others, or you experience stress, or you get ulcers, or a skin rash, or any number of other maladies. What is the price you pay for wearing the mask?

(Pause for thirty seconds).

All right, is the reason that you wear this mask still valid? Is it really valid? And what is the worst that would happen if you were to remove the mask and be who you really are?

(Pause for forty seconds.)

All right, remember everything you're perceiving, but it's time to move on and explore another mask. This time a mask that relates to your primary relationship. Or to your relationship with someone who is important to you. Take a moment to think about a primary mask you wear with this important person.

(Pause for forty seconds.)

All right, behind all repression, all masks, there is fear. In this case, what is the fear that keeps you from being who you really are?

(Pause for thirty seconds.)

And now, what is the price you pay for wearing the mask?

(Pause for thirty seconds.)

OK ... is the reason you wear this mask still valid? What is the worst that would happen if you were to remove the mask and be who you really are?

(Pause for forty seconds.)

All right, now let's explore another mask. This time a mask that relates to your career. Take a few moments and think about an important career mask.

(Pause for thirty seconds.)

OK ... what is the fear behind the mask?

(Pause for thirty seconds.)

And what is the price you pay for wearing this mask?

(Pause for thirty seconds.)

Is this mask still valid? What is the worst that would happen if you were to remove the mask and be who you really are?

(Pause for thirty seconds.)

All right, are there any additional masks that you feel would be of value to explore? Social masks, sexual masks, spiritual masks, or masks that you feel are forced upon you by the demands of society? Take a few minutes to meditate upon any of these masks you recognize in your life. Explore the fears behind them, the price of wearing them ... and explore what would happen if you were to remove them once and for all.

(Pause for four minutes.)

I hope that you now have more understanding of repression and masks. It's important to remember that nothing about us can be changed until it is first accepted. You created your masks to keep out pain, but the masks have also kept you from experiencing your full potential of joy.

You have the power and ability to create your own reality, to change what isn't working and to manifest what you desire.

In just a moment, I'm going to wake you up. On the count of five, you will open your eyes and be wide awake, fully alert, thinking and acting with calm self-assurance. You'll awaken feeling as if you've just taken a relaxing nap, and you'll be at peace with yourself, the world, and everyone in it.

Number one, coming on up now and feeling an expanding spiritual light within.

Number two, coming up feeling at peace with all life.

Number three, coming on up and tapping into an internal balance and harmony.

Number four, recall the situation in the room.

And number five, wide awake, wide awake. Open your eyes and feel good. Number five, wide awake.

The Pain Control Process

You're breathing deeply and relaxing completely.

Breathing deeply and relaxing completely . . . and allowing a quietness of spirit to come in. Taking a deep breath in and holding it as long as you comfortably can . . . then let the breath out slowly through slightly parted lips, and when the breath is all the way out, push it further out, and further out . . . and then repeat the process. Breathing deeply, and when any outside thoughts come into your mind, simply brush them aside and tell yourself, "I'll deal with that later," and then return your concentration to the sound of my voice, and breathing deeply and relaxing completely.

And in just a moment I'm going to relax your body one part at a time. So play the role, play the part, and feel your body relaxing as I ask you to do so. And the relaxing power is coming into the toes of both of your feet at the same time . . . and it's moving right on down into the balls of your feet, into your arches, into your heels, and right on up to your ankles. Completely relaxed, completely relaxed . . . and the relaxing sensations now move on up your legs to your knees, relaxing all the muscles as it goes. And on up your legs now, to your thighs and to your hips. Permeating every cell and every atom.

And you're relaxing completely, relaxing completely, keeping your full attention on the sound of my voice and relaxing your body, as the relaxing sensations move on down into the fingers of both of your hands ... relaxing your hands. Feel your hands relaxing. And your lower arms are relaxed, and your upper arms are relaxed. Fingers and hands and lower arms and upper arms ... just completely relaxed.

And the relaxing sensations now move on down into the base of your spine, your root chakra. Imagine a warmth in your root chakra as if a ray of sunlight were coming into the room and falling upon your spine ... and it feels good. You imagine this warmth now moving up your spine ... up your spine ... up your spine and into the back of your neck and shoulder muscles. And your shoulder muscles are now loose and limp ... loose and limp ... just completely relaxed. And the relaxing sensations now move on up the back of your neck and into your scalp. Relaxing your scalp. Feel your scalp relaxing, and feel the relaxing sensations now drain down into your facial muscles, relaxing your facial muscles. Your jaw is relaxed. Allow a little space between your teeth. And your throat is relaxed. Your entire body is now relaxed all over in every way. And all tension is gone from your body and mind.

And as you continue to focus upon the sound of my voice, I am going to count you down, down, down ... so vividly imagine yourself in a situation going down ... walking down stairs, downhill, down the side of a pyramid ... or any situation in which you see yourself going down, while I count backwards from seven to one.

Number seven, deeper, deeper, deeper, down, down, down.

Number six, deeper, deeper, deeper, down, down, down.

Number five, deeper, deeper, deeper, down, down, down.

Number four, deeper, deeper, deeper, down, down, down.

Number three, deeper, deeper, deeper, down, down, down.

Number two, deeper, deeper, deeper, down, down, down.

Number one, deeper, deeper, deeper, down, down, down.

And you're relaxed and at ease, and you feel deep. But let's go down a little deeper now . . . deeper now.

Number seven, deeper, deeper, deeper, down, down, down.

Number six, deeper, deeper, deeper, down, down, down.

Number five, deeper, deeper, deeper, down, down, down.

Number four, deeper, deeper, deeper, down, down, down.

Number three, deeper, deeper, deeper, down, down, down.

Number two, deeper, deeper, deeper, down, down, down.

Number one, deeper, deeper, deeper, down, down, down.

And you're now relaxed and at ease, and you can awaken at any time by simply counting up from one to five and saying the words, "Wide awake." So you're in control of this mind-programming session. And I'm going to begin by providing suggestions which will be communicated to every level of your body and mind, and they'll be accepted on every level of your body and mind.

Your muscles are relaxed, and your mind is at ease. You have the power and ability to block any sensations you don't want to feel. You do. You accept this.

Focusing the unlimited power of your mind, you can send numbing sensations into any discomfort.

You block all physical sensations you don't want to experience. You have this power.

You block what you don't want to feel.

Allow it to happen. Feel it happening.

You obtain relief when you desire to obtain relief.

Your mind is in control of your body.

You feel better, and better, and better.

Your entire body is relaxed all over in every way, and you're feeling better and better and better.

The word *anesthesia* is your key trigger word for post-hypnotic conditioned response.

And these suggestions have been communicated to every level of your body and mind, and they've been accepted on every level of your body and mind, and so it is.

And you know that you must only use this pain control technique when you know the cause. You will also consult a doctor if the condition persists.

It's now time to invoke a technique called *glove anesthesia*. And we'll begin by concentrating upon your dominant hand, which is beginning to lose all feeling. It's all right.

Focus your attention upon your hand, and allow it to lose all feeling. You hand is becoming numb. No feeling at all. No feeling at all. But I'd like you to help out here, by mentally telling your hand to go to sleep. Tell it to go to sleep. Go to sleep. Your hand is going to sleep. It becomes numb. No feeling at all. No feeling at all. And every breath you take seems to cause your hand to become number, and number, and number, until you just can't feel your hand at all. You just can't feel your hand at all because it is numb. Numb. No feeling. Numb. No feeling. No feeling.

And now . . . you're going to transfer this lack of feeling to the part of your body that you desire to feel numb. So on the count of three, you're going to raise your hand and place it upon the part of your body you want to feel numb. And in so doing, you'll transfer this numbness to that portion of your body.

So get ready now . . . on the count of three, raise your hand and touch the part of your body you want to become cool and numb. Number one . . . number two . . . and number three. Release the numbness into another part of your body. Move your hand and transfer the numbness.

(Pause for thirty seconds.)

And you've now transferred the calming, soothing, numbing coolness, and you're physically feeling better and better and better. Settling down to normal, and the coolness permeates the area. You experience wonderful relief. All the tension is gone from your body and mind, and you breathe deeply and relax completely, feeling better and better. Calm, cool, soothing, numbing sensations permeate the area.

Better and better. Numbness. Relief. Numbness. Relief.

And it's time to focus the incredible power of visualization by imagining yourself having already resolved your current condition and feeling good all the time. You physically feel as good as you've ever felt, and you experience joy in this realization. Create every detail of this visualization, including your reaction and the reactions of others. And in so doing, you communicate your desire to the levels of mind that will assist you in manifesting the positive outcome. Visualize now while I'm quiet for awhile.

(Pause for ninety seconds.)

And you've just seen your own reality. You have the power and ability to create your own reality. You do, and you accept this. You experience this. And every day in every way, you become more powerful in your ability to control your physical and mental reactions to any condition. You know that you must only use this pain control technique when you know the cause. You will also consult a doctor if the condition persists.

And you are open and accepting of positive suggestions which you will consciously and unconsciously act upon.

Your muscles are relaxed and your mind is at ease.

You have the power and ability to block any sensations you do not want to feel. You do. You accept this.

Focusing the unlimited power of your mind, you can send numbing sensations into any discomfort.

You block all physical sensations you don't want to experience. You can. You accept this.

You block what you don't want to feel.

Allow it to happen. Feel it happening.

You obtain relief when you desire to obtain relief.

Your mind is in control of your body.

You feel better, and better, and better.

Your entire body is relaxed all over in every way, and you're feeling better and better and better.

The word *anesthesia* is your key trigger word for post-hypnotic conditioned response.

And these suggestions have been communicated to every level of your body and mind, and they've been accepted on every level of your body and mind, and so it is.

And I'm now going to give you a key trigger word for posthypnotic conditioned response. Any time you begin to feel discomfort, you will simply stop what you're doing, close your eyes, breathe deeply, and say this word quietly to yourself . . . *anesthesia*. The word *anesthesia* is a conditioned response key to your subconscious mind, and when you say *anesthesia*, you will draw upon the unlimited power of your mind to control physical sensations. When you say *anesthesia*, you will feel the cooling numbness you experienced earlier in this session spreading to the part of your body in need of relief. The word *anesthesia* now becomes your key for totally effective conditioned response, and every time you hear this suggestion and every time you use your *anesthesia* programming, it will become more and more effective.

And now, once again, it's time to create another visualization in which you perceive yourself feeling good all the time. You feel as good as you've ever felt, and you experience joy in this realization. Imagine yourself doing what you most love to do. Create every detail of this visualization.

In so doing, you communicate your desires to the mental levels that have the power to assist you in manifesting the positive outcome. Visualize now while I'm quiet for awhile.

(Pause for ninety seconds.)

And you've just seen your own reality, and upon awakening, you'll remember all that has been communicated. You'll awaken feeling as if you just had a refreshing nap. Your head will be clear, and you'll think and act with calm self-assurance . . . feeling glad to be alive and at peace with yourself the world and everyone in it. So let's come on up now. On the count of five, you'll open your eyes and be wide awake.

Number one, feel the life blood returning to your arms and legs.

Number two, coming on up and at peace with all life.

Number three, coming on up feeling an internal balance and harmony.

Number four, recall the situation and the room.

Number five, wide awake, wide awake. Open your eyes and feel good. Number five, wide awake.

Parallel Lives

The concept of simultaneous multiple incarnations explains how reincarnation really works and resolves the conflicts that this concept appears to raise.

Both Dick and Jane Roberts (in the Seth books) wrote about parallel lives—the fact that you are more than one person now living on the earth. In his seminars, Dick conducted parallel lives sessions with thousands of people, and everyone was always able to perceive these ties, just as everyone can recall past lives in regression. Your "oversoul" created you and two or three others as an extension of energy-expanding potential. If you're interested in reincarnation, this course will resolve the inconsistencies, and it may explain some of the situations in your life, such as why you are drawn to a subject, or why you may have been depressed during a period of your life. This is the outer edge of metaphysical study, and New Agers will be well served by these explorations.

Some statisticians say that there are nearly as many people now living on the earth as the sum total of all the people who have ever lived. So there are not enough past lives to go around. In response, Dick began with a concept that's difficult for many people to grasp: *You are more than one person now living on the earth.*

While Dick was writing his book *You Were Born Again to Be Together*, he met Alex, who asked him to conduct a hypnosis session. Alex had experienced several dreams in which he saw his wife, Louise, in an unfamiliar modern setting, but she looked different. Through hypnosis and working with a trance channel, we discovered that Louise, who lived in Phoenix, Arizona, was also a woman named Mary living on a farm in Iowa.

David Paladin, the channeler who helped Dick investigate this case said, "There is a union between the women in sleep, and often the thoughts of one are known in the mind of the other, but are considered their own."

Over time, lying side by side in sleep, couples tend to align their brain wave frequencies, which creates a psychic link. While dreaming, Alex was drawing images from his wife's mind—images of her parallel self in Iowa.

You Were Born Again to Be Together was first published in April 1976. In the fall of 1976, Jane Roberts' book of Seth channeling entitled *Psychic Politics* was published. Although Dick did not see Jane's manuscript and she didn't see his, they were writing about the same thing. Seth said, "You can live more than one life in one time. You are neurologically turned in to one particular field of actuality that you recognize."

Here is another excerpt from *Psychic Politics*:

SETH: If you could think of a multidimensional body existing at one time in different realities, and appearing differently within those realities, then you could get a glimpse of what is involved. . . .

You live more than one life at a time. You do not experience your century simply from one separate vantage point, and the individuals alive in any given century have far deeper connections than you realize. You do not experience your space-time world, then, from one but from many viewpoints.

Case Histories

The following is an interesting case history from *You Were Born Again to Be Together*: Cherry Hartman, a psychiatric social worker for Lutheran Family Services, received answers to all of the questions Dick had asked of the hypnotized seminar participants in a group parallel-life transference session. Instead of sharing lunch with the group, she spent her lunch hour on the phone attempting to verify what she learned in hypnosis. After lunch, Cherry shared what she learned.

She said, "In the parallel-life transfer, I went into a lifetime as James Arthur Phelps. I was an encyclopedia salesman, and the year was 1963. I perceived the full address, city, and state. My wife's name was Jackie. I checked this out with the help of the telephone operator and found the address to be real, but there is no one by that name living there now. I was able to talk to a woman who lives a few houses away and she told me that a Phelps family had lived on the block ten years ago. Also, she verified the wife's name."

Were Cherry Hartman and James Arthur Phelps parallels—extensions of the same oversoul? Dick believed so, and Cherry believed this to be the case as well.

A twenty-eight-year-old female seminar participant shared this story after the transfer session: "I went back, or went over and found myself twelve years in the past. My name is Johanna Harris, and I live in Peru. I'm a nurse, and the only way you can get to where I am is on the riverboat that brings supplies, which we get once a month. The village that I live in—there's two very large huts . . . grass type huts and there's four or five smaller ones for the individual people. My hobbies are the children of the village. I also go hunting for rocks and gems, getting off in the jungle by myself.

"As Johanna, I happen to be handling people in the hospital that can't do for themselves. They can't move themselves, and the chief of the village especially . . . he's a large man and he's very heavy to try to move."

She paused in sharing her story, placed a hand on her lower back and said, "Maybe this explains why my back hurts sometimes."

The following response was from a thirty-nine-year-old seminar participant who experienced the Parallel Lives Transfer session. She cried as she told her story: "I got very brief information, but I first picked up on a parallel at age nine. She was born approximately nine months after I was in the same town, Philadelphia . . . the same hospital, and her name was Susan. She was living in Detroit at the age of nine, near Lake Michigan. Then this other information started coming in. It was a real shocker. In 1962 she lost a child that I birthed in December of '62. There is other cross-tie information I can't share with the group for personal reasons. In 1975, Susan was involved in a sailing accident that crippled her and eventually led to her death in October of last year. Well, I know that all of this has had a lot to do with my own depressed state of mind during the months she suffered. I got this out of it. I can describe the house she lived in. It was frame, one story with a basement—Victorian style . . . and white with blue trim on the outside."

A forty-eight-year-old male seminar attendee who participated in a group parallel-life transference session shared this:

"If I can accept this, I am also a doctor practicing in New York City. I couldn't get his name, but I guarantee you I'd recognize his offices if I were to ever see them. I saw the office door with many names on it, but they were fuzzy. Anyway, I'm probably in my late fifties or early sixties and have three grown children. My wife died several years ago, and I'm now living alone in an apartment in Manhattan. An interesting fact here is that in my own reality, I was a medic in the war, was good at it, and learned quickly, but I saw enough human suffering to last me a lifetime. After the war, I started my own manufacturing business instead of pursuing medicine . . . at least this part of me did."

Parallel Life Transfer Session

You're breathing deeply and relaxing completely.

Breathing deeply and relaxing completely . . . and allowing a quietness of spirit to come in. Taking a deep breath in and holding it as long as you comfortably can . . . then let the breath out slowly through slightly parted lips, and when the breath is all the way out, push it further out, and further out . . . and then repeat the process. Breathing deeply, and when any outside thoughts come into your mind, simply brush them aside and tell yourself, "I'll deal with that later," and then return your concentration to the sound of my voice, and breathing deeply and relaxing completely.

And in just a moment I'm going to relax your body one part at a time. So play the role, play the part, and feel your body relaxing as I ask you to do so. And the relaxing power is coming into the toes of both of your feet at the same time . . . and it's moving right on down into the balls of your feet, into your arches, into your heels, and right on up to your ankles. Completely relaxed, completely relaxed . . . and the relaxing sensations now move on up your legs to your knees, relaxing all the muscles as it goes. And on up your legs now, to your thighs and to your hips. Permeating every cell and every atom.

And you're relaxing completely, relaxing completely, keeping your full attention on the sound of my voice and relaxing your body, as the relaxing sensations move on down into the fingers of both of your hands . . . relaxing your hands. Feel your hands relaxing. And your lower arms are relaxed, and your upper arms are relaxed. Fingers and hands and lower arms and upper arms . . . just completely relaxed.

And the relaxing sensations now move on down into the base of your spine, your root chakra. Imagine a warmth in your root chakra as if a ray of sunlight were coming into the room and falling upon your spine . . . and it feels good. You imagine this warmth now moving up your spine . . . up your spine . . . up your spine and into the back of your

neck and shoulder muscles. And your shoulder muscles are now loose and limp . . . loose and limp . . . just completely relaxed. And the relaxing sensations now move on up the back of your neck and into your scalp. Relaxing your scalp. Feel your scalp relaxing, and feel the relaxing sensations now drain down into your facial muscles, relaxing your facial muscles. Your jaw is relaxed. Allow a little space between your teeth. And your throat is relaxed. Your entire body is now relaxed all over in every way. And all tension is gone from your body and mind.

And we're now going to balance and energize your aura and attune you to the subtle vibrations that support the perception of subjective awareness. So to begin, imagine a beam of iridescent white light coming down from above and entering your crown chakra of spirituality on the top of your head. Imagine the light . . . create it with the unlimited power of your mind. This is the Universal light of life energy, and you feel it stimulating this chakra center, which is purple in color. Visualize a swirling vortex of purple, and the light opens, balances, and charges this chakra center. Imagine the opening, balancing, charging.

(Pause for five seconds.)

And the light is now moving on down into the center of your forehead—your brow chakra, which is a swirling blue-violet vortex of energy. Perceive the blue-violet color, and feel the balancing and energizing that is taking place here.

Opening, balancing, energizing.

(Pause for five seconds.)

And the light is now moving on down into your throat chakra, which is a swirling silvery-blue vortex of energy.

Perceive the silvery-blue color, and feel the balancing and energizing that is taking place here. Opening, balancing, energizing.

(Pause for five seconds.)

And the light is now moving on down into your heart chakra, which is to be perceived as a golden glow. Perceive the golden color, and feel the balancing and energizing of your heart chakra center. Opening, balancing, energizing.

(Pause for five seconds.)

And the light is now moving on down into your solar plexus chakra, located at the level of your navel. This chakra is to be visualized as several shades of red in color. Perceive the red colors, and imagine the balancing and energizing that is taking place here. Opening, balancing, energizing.

(Pause for five seconds.)

And the light is moving on down into your sacral or spleen chakra, which is located a little below your navel. This swirling vortex of energy is a rainbow of colors. Perceive the many colors, and feel the balancing and energizing that is taking place here. Opening, balancing, energizing.

(Pause for five seconds.)

And the light is now moving on down into your root chakra at the base of your spine. This chakra is to be visualized as a swirling vortex of energy, red and orange in color. Perceive the reds and oranges, and feel the balancing and energizing that is taking place here. Opening, balancing, energizing.

(Pause for five seconds.)

And your chakras are opened, balanced, and charged, thus expanding your aura and attuning you to the subtle vibrations that support the perception of subjective awareness.

And it's now time to imagine the bright white light moving back up into heart area. Visualize your heart center overflowing with the Universal light of life energy.

And now imagine the light emerging from your heart center to surround your body in a protective aura of bright white God light.

And you are totally protected. Totally protected. Only your own Guides and Masters or highly evolved and loving entities who mean you well will be able to influence you in any way in this altered state of consciousness session.

And as you continue to focus upon the sound of my voice, I am going to count you down, down, down . . . so vividly imagine yourself in a situation going down . . . walking down stairs, downhill, down the side of a pyramid . . . or any situation in which you see yourself going down, while I count backwards from seven to one.

Number seven, deeper, deeper, deeper, down, down, down.

Number six, deeper, deeper, deeper, down, down, down.

Number five, deeper, deeper, deeper, down, down, down.

Number four, deeper, deeper, deeper, down, down, down.

Number three, deeper, deeper, deeper, down, down, down.

Number two, deeper, deeper, deeper, down, down, down. Number one, deeper, deeper, deeper, down, down, down.

And you're relaxed and at ease, and you feel deep. But let's go down a little deeper now . . . deeper now.

Number seven, deeper, deeper, deeper, down, down, down.

Number six, deeper, deeper, deeper, down, down, down.

Number five, deeper, deeper, deeper, down, down, down.

Number four, deeper, deeper, deeper, down, down, down.

Number three, deeper, deeper, deeper, down, down, down.

Number two, deeper, deeper, deeper, down, down, down. Number one, deeper, deeper, deeper, down, down, down.

You're relaxed and at ease, and a quietness of spirit now permeates your body and mind. And we're now going to work together to establish a tie between you and another individual who is also you . . . a parallel life . . . Your soul or oversoul may be exploring more than one potential on the earth at this time. You may also be other individuals now living, or individuals who have crossed over but once lived within the physical time frame of your life—from your birth up until this very moment. You may be a baby living somewhere in the world, and a male rancher down in Mexico, and a female painter living in France. There are as many possibilities as there are people who have lived during your lifetime.

Now if indeed you are experiencing other explorations of potential in other bodies, your own Higher Self is fully aware of this. You only use 10 percent of your mental ability, but you can use more. Much more. Within the 90 percent you do not normally use is a level of understanding that's always aware of all that relates to you. And you can tap into this awareness if you will simply trust the impressions that flow into your mind when we complete a transfer.

And we're now going to seek to establish a tie with another entity who is also of your lineage—an extension of the same soul or oversoul. You have the power and ability to allow a mental transference to take place. You will ideally perceive an aspect of your parallel's life that will assist you to better understand yourself.

(Pause for five seconds.)

You may observe through your parallel self's eyes, or you may find yourself observing them much as you would while standing in a room observing another person. In this process, while you will be able to see them, you will be invisible to them. All you have to do is *trust* your perceptions. Trust every thought, feeling, and visualization.

(Pause for five seconds.)

So . . . if there is now, or has ever been, an extension of your soul living upon the earth during your lifespan, you will transfer in time and space to observe them. If you have several parallel selves, you will transfer to the one most influential to you. You may transfer in the present, or you may go back in time to a situation in your parallel's life that will help you better understand the soul union you share.

(Pause for five seconds.)

All right, it's time to imagine a tunnel with your inner eyes. This is a tunnel through time and space, and it can be any kind of tunnel you care to imagine . . . so vividly imagine the tunnel . . . and perceive yourself stepping into the tunnel and beginning to transfer in time and space as I count from five to one. On the count of one, you will step out of the end of the tunnel and perceive your parallel self.

Number five, you're in the tunnel and beginning to move through time and space. Allow it to happen. Feel it happening. You're just letting go and moving through the tunnel now . . . moving toward that light way down at the end . . .

Number four, moving through the tunnel to activate the transfer . . . transcending time and space to better understand your totality . . .

Number three, moving through the tunnel to explore one of your parallel lives . . . and you're getting closer and closer and closer to the light at the end . . .

Number two, you're almost there, almost there. And on the next count, you will step out of the end of the tunnel and begin to observe another aspect of your totality . . .

And number one . . . you're now there. Step out of the tunnel and allow impressions to begin to form.

All right . . . you're now in the presence of your parallel self.

So look around and perceive their presence.

(Pause for twenty seconds.)

Do you sense you're outdoors or indoors? If you're outdoors, perceive the environment. If you sense you're indoors, perceive the room and any furnishings, windows or doorways.

(Pause for twenty seconds.)

And now, vividly perceive your parallel self. Imagine how they look . . . Are they male or female? . . . About how old do you judge them to be at this time?

(Pause for forty seconds.)

All right, it's time to become aware of the year in which you're observing your parallel self. So simply trust as the numbers of the year come into your mind. The first number of the year is . . . ? Second number? . . . Third number? . . . And the fourth number? . . . And you should now have the year.

And now, let's explore the location, the country and city, or nearest city, if possible. So allow this information to simply come into your mind, or trust as letters form one at a time, spelling out the location. Do this on your own.

(Pause for forty seconds.)

You should now have the location . . . And it's time to move around in time and space, so let's explore the most important event that has ever taken place in your parallel's life. On the count of three, you'll move in time and observe this important situation. Number one, number two, and number three.

(Pause for sixty seconds.)

All right . . . now remember everything you're observing, but it's time to find out what your parallel does for a living, their career or the primary way that they spend their time. Vivid impressions will come into your mind on the count of three.

Number one, number two, and number three.

(Pause for sixty seconds.)

OK . . . remember what you're observing, but let go. It's time to learn how your parallel is most influencing you.

Since there is a superconscious connection between the two of you, your parallel self may have interests, learned abilities, or talents that you're perceiving through Higher Mind. Vivid impressions of what your parallel does that influences you will come in on the count of three. Number one, number two, number three.

(Pause for sixty seconds.)

All right . . . it's time to perceive how someone could make contact with your parallel, so be totally open and trusting now . . . and this information will come in on the count of three. Number one, number two, and number three.

(Pause for sixty seconds.)

And now take some time to look around your parallel's house or apartment to see if you can gather information that would help you to locate your parallel self. As an example, you might notice an address on an envelope, or an address label on a magazine.

(Pause for sixty seconds.)

OK . . . it's time for you to ask your own questions and receive your own answers with thought language. Simply ask a question with a thought, and then listen for your answer as a returning thought. Do this on your own now.

(Pause for three minutes.)

All right . . . it's now time to let go of this, but you'll remember everything you have experienced while observing your parallel self. You can always return to further explore your personal world of parallel lives, but on the count of three you'll be back in the present, with your eyes closed, in a peaceful altered state of consciousness. So come on back now, number one, number two, and number three.

And in just a moment I'm going to wake you up. On the count of five, you will open your eyes and be wide awake, fully alert, thinking and acting with calm self-assurance. You'll awaken feeling as if you've just taken a relaxing nap, and you'll be at peace with yourself, the world, and everyone in it.

Number one, coming on up now and feeling an expanding spiritual light within.

Number two, coming up feeling at peace with all life.

Number three, coming on up and tapping into an internal balance and harmony.

Number four, recall the situation in the room.

And number five, wide awake, wide awake. Open your eyes and feel good. Number five, wide awake.

Personality Aspects

We all contain many subpersonalities that have manifested as a result of past experiences and conflicting desires, plus identification with particular archetypes.

The idea of this session is to directly communicate with some of the personality aspects currently directing your life. You can easily do this, because you can just make up the communications. You can imagine what you hear with your inner ears or feel is being expressed. If you can trust yourself to do this, the words may just take off on their own. And by trusting your thoughts, you will soon be receiving valuable information.

I'll direct various aspects of your personality to dialogue with you. If you want, you can visualize each aspect in some appropriate form ... maybe as a person, an animal, or a symbol.

Here are some of the most common subpersonalities:

- The Critic
- The Judge
- The Moralist
- The Preacher
- The Hero/Heroine
- The Attention Seeker
- The Sympathy Seeker
- The Pleaser
- The Brute
- The Helpless One
- The Aggressor
- The Dominant One

- The Organizer
- The Sadist
- The Masochist
- The Sexist
- The Insecure One
- The Important One
- The Clown
- The Victim
- The Manipulator
- The Martyr
- The Nag
- The Tightwad
- The Lover
- The Romantic
- The Prude
- The Provider
- The Protector
- The Responsible One
- The Entertainer
- The Star
- The Greedy One
- The Selfish One
- The Bitch
- The Skeptic
- The Bragger

Subpersonality Hypnosis Session

You're breathing deeply and relaxing completely.

Breathing deeply and relaxing completely . . . and allowing a quietness of spirit to come in. Taking a deep breath in and holding it as long as you comfortably can . . . then let the breath out slowly through slightly parted lips, and when the breath is all the way out, push it further out, and further out . . . and then repeat the process. Breathing deeply, and when any outside thoughts come into your mind, simply brush them aside and tell yourself, "I'll deal with that later," and then return your concentration to the sound of my voice, and breathing deeply and relaxing completely.

And in just a moment, I'm going to relax your body one part at a time. So play the role, play the part, and feel your body relaxing as I ask you to do so. And the relaxing power is coming into the toes of both of your feet at the same time . . . and it's moving right on down into the balls of your feet, into your arches, into your heels, and right on up to your ankles. Completely relaxed, completely relaxed . . . and the relaxing sensations now move on up your legs to your knees, relaxing all the muscles as it goes. And on up your legs now, to your thighs and to your hips. Permeating every cell and every atom.

And you're relaxing completely, relaxing completely, keeping your full attention on the sound of my voice and relaxing your body, as the relaxing sensations move on down into the fingers of both of your hands . . . relaxing your hands. Feel your hands relaxing. And your lower arms are relaxed, and your upper arms are relaxed. Fingers and hands and lower arms and upper arms . . . just completely relaxed.

And the relaxing sensations now move on down into the base of your spine, your root chakra. Imagine a warmth in your root chakra as if a ray of sunlight were coming into the room and falling upon your spine . . . and it feels good. You imagine this warmth now moving up your spine . . . up your spine . . . up your spine and into the back of your neck and shoulder muscles. And your shoulder muscles are now loose and limp . . . loose and limp . . . just completely relaxed. And the relaxing sensations now move on up the back of your neck and into your scalp. Relaxing your scalp. Feel your scalp relaxing, and feel the relaxing sensations now drain down into your facial muscles, relaxing your facial muscles. Your jaw is relaxed. Allow a little space between your teeth. And your throat is relaxed. Your entire body is now relaxed all over in every way. And all tension is gone from your body and mind.

And we're now going to balance and energize your aura and attune you to the subtle vibrations that support the perception of subjective awareness. So to begin, imagine a beam of iridescent white light coming down from above and entering your crown chakra of spirituality on the top of your head. Imagine the light . . . create it with the unlimited power of your mind. This is the Universal light of life energy, and you feel it stimulating this chakra center, which is purple in color. Visualize a swirling vortex of purple, and the light opens, balances, and charges this chakra center. Imagine the opening, balancing, charging.

(Pause for five seconds.)

And the light is now moving on down into the center of your forehead—your brow chakra, which is a swirling blue-violet vortex of energy. Perceive the blue-violet color, and feel the balancing and energizing that is taking place here.

Opening, balancing, energizing.

(Pause for five seconds.)

And the light is now moving on down into your throat chakra, which is a swirling silvery-blue vortex of energy.

Perceive the silvery-blue color, and feel the balancing and energizing that is taking place here. Opening, balancing, energizing.

(Pause for five seconds.)

And the light is now moving on down into your heart chakra, which is to be perceived as a golden glow. Perceive the golden color, and feel the balancing and energizing of your heart chakra center. Opening, balancing, energizing.

(Pause for five seconds.)

And the light is now moving on down into your solar plexus chakra, located at the level of your navel. This chakra is to be visualized as several shades of red in color. Perceive the red colors, and imagine the balancing and energizing that is taking place here. Opening, balancing, energizing.

(Pause for five seconds.)

And the light is moving on down into your sacral or spleen chakra, which is located a little below your navel. This swirling vortex of energy is a rainbow of colors. Perceive the many colors, and feel the balancing and energizing that is taking place here. Opening, balancing, energizing.

(Pause for five seconds.)

And the light is now moving on down into your root chakra at the base of your spine. This chakra is to be visualized as a swirling vortex of energy, red and orange in color. Perceive the reds and oranges, and feel the balancing and energizing that is taking place here. Opening, balancing, energizing.

(Pause for five seconds.)

And your chakras are opened, balanced, and charged, thus expanding your aura and attuning you to the subtle vibrations that support the perception of subjective awareness.

And it's now time to imagine the bright white light moving back up into heart area. Visualize your heart center overflowing with the Universal light of life energy. And now imagine the light emerging from your heart center to surround your body in a protective aura of bright white God light. And you are totally protected. Totally protected. Only your own Guides and Masters or highly evolved and loving entities who mean you well will be able to influence you in any way in this altered state of consciousness session.

And as you continue to focus upon the sound of my voice, I am going to count you down, down, down . . . so vividly imagine yourself in a situation going down . . . walking down stairs, downhill, down the side of a pyramid . . . or any situation in which you see yourself going down, while I count backwards from seven to one.

Number seven, deeper, deeper, deeper, down, down, down.

Number six, deeper, deeper, deeper, down, down, down.

Number five, deeper, deeper, deeper, down, down, down.

Number four, deeper, deeper, deeper, down, down, down.

Number three, deeper, deeper, deeper, down, down, down.

Number two, deeper, deeper, deeper, down, down, down.

Number one, deeper, deeper, deeper, down, down, down.

And you're relaxed and at ease, and you feel deep. But let's go down a little deeper now . . . deeper now.

Number seven, deeper, deeper, deeper, down, down, down.

Number six, deeper, deeper, deeper, down, down, down.
Number five, deeper, deeper, deeper, down, down, down.
Number four, deeper, deeper, deeper, down, down, down.
Number three, deeper, deeper, deeper, down, down, down.

Number two, deeper, deeper, deeper, down, down, down. Number one, deeper, deeper, deeper, down, down, down.

And you're now relaxed and at ease, and a quietness of spirit fills your body and mind. And in just a moment we're going to begin to work together to attain a better understanding of yourself.

(Pause for ten seconds.)

All right now, it's time to allow this aspect to express itself through your hand. Write down everything you perceive. Why does the aspect feel repressed, and what would it like to have happen? And it's time to just barely open your eyes and position your pen to paper and begin to write. Allow this repressed aspect to write.

(Pause for ninety seconds.)

OK . . . let go of this now . . . and it's time to draw a defiant aspect of your totality into the light. There is within you a defiant aspect of your totality that needs to come forward and express itself. Bring out this defiant, resistant aspect.

(Pause for ten seconds.)

And now, allow this aspect to express itself through your hand. Write down everything you perceive. Why does the aspect feel defiant or resistant? What is it the aspect doesn't like? What would it like to have happen? Allow the writing to come through.

(Pause for ninety seconds.)

OK . . . let's let go of this now . . . and it's time to draw an aspect retaining old emotional pain into the light. There is a part of you that still feels wounded by old pain. Bring out this hurt aspect of your totality.

(Pause for ten seconds.)

All right . . . now it's time to allow this aspect to express itself through your hand. Write down everything you perceive. Why does this aspect retain the pain, and what would it like to have happen? Begin writing.

(Pause for ninety seconds.)

OK . . . let go of this now . . . and it's time to draw an aspect that judges and blames others to come forward into the light. Allow this judging, blaming aspect to appear so it can express itself.

(Pause for ten seconds.)

All right, now allow this aspect to express itself through your hand. Write down everything you perceive. Why does the aspect judge and blame?

(Pause for ninety seconds.)

All right, now within you are aspects that want to get well, and maybe aspects that don't want to get well. So we'll begin with the aspect that does not want to get well. Draw it out into the light so it can express itself through your hand. Write everything you perceive. Why doesn't this aspect want to get well? Explore all the reasoning and any benefits derived from remaining as you are.

(Pause for ninety seconds.)

All right . . . let go of this, and let's now draw the primary aspect that wants to get well into the light so that it can express itself. Write down everything you perceive. Explore this energy and support for wellness.

(Pause for ninety seconds.)

OK . . . it's time to let go of this and draw an aspect that denies reality to come forward into the light so that it can express itself. Write down everything you perceive from this aspect that cannot accept what is.

(Pause for ninety seconds.)

OK ... let go of this now ... and it's time for you to directly communicate with Higher Mind about what you should be doing mentally, physically, emotionally, and spiritually. Write down everything you perceive from your Higher Mind.

(Pause for ninety seconds.)

And it's time to awaken, remembering everything that you've just experienced ... feeling glad to be alive and at peace with yourself, the world, and everyone in it.

And in just a moment I'm going to wake you up. On the count of five, you will open your eyes and be wide awake, fully alert, thinking and acting with calm self-assurance. You'll awaken feeling as if you've just taken a relaxing nap, and you'll be at peace with yourself, the world, and everyone in it.

Number one, coming on up now and feeling an expanding spiritual light within.

Number two, coming up feeling at peace with all life.

Number three, coming on up and tapping into an internal balance and harmony.

Number four, recall the situation in the room.

And number five, wide awake, wide awake. Open your eyes and feel good. Number five, wide awake.

Prebirth Planning

Between lifetimes, we rest, work, and prepare to reincarnate. Master teachers—highly evolved souls—will gather with an entity to plot needed lessons for the next incarnation. This includes the entity's involvement with hundreds of other souls who will incarnate within the same time frame, and all the karmic interactions to generate learning opportunities. Astrology, the exact moment and place of birth, sets the soul on a path that will serve as a blueprint for the earth life.

This Prebirth Planning session is part of the cycle of rebirth for every individual. The Master teachers do not tell you what you are to encounter in the new life. They suggest, but you always have the free will to override the suggestions. After forty years of research, Dick concluded that most people tend to be very brave in spirit. They believe that they've learned their lessons from the mistakes of prior lifetimes and are anxious to take on the mantle of a human body to balance their karma and test themselves once again.

Prebirth Planning Session

You're breathing deeply and relaxing completely.

Breathing deeply and relaxing completely . . . and allowing a quietness of spirit to come in. Taking a deep breath in and holding it as long as you comfortably can . . . then let the breath out slowly through slightly parted lips, and when the breath is all the way out, push it further out, and further out . . . and then repeat the process. Breathing deeply, and when any outside thoughts come into your mind, simply brush them aside and tell yourself, "I'll deal with that later," and then return your concentration to the sound of my voice, and breathing deeply and relaxing completely.

And in just a moment I'm going to relax your body one part at a time. So play the role, play the part, and feel your body relaxing as I ask you to do so. And the relaxing power is coming into the toes of both of your feet at the same time . . . and it's moving right on down into the balls of your feet, into your arches, into your heels, and right on up to your ankles. Completely relaxed, completely relaxed . . . and the relaxing sensations now move on up your legs to your knees, relaxing all the muscles as it goes. And on up your legs now, to your thighs and to your hips. Permeating every cell and every atom.

And you're relaxing completely, relaxing completely, keeping your full attention on the sound of my voice and relaxing your body, as the relaxing sensations move on down into the fingers of both of your hands . . . relaxing your hands. Feel your hands relaxing. And your lower arms are relaxed, and your upper arms are relaxed. Fingers and hands and lower arms and upper arms . . . just completely relaxed.

And the relaxing sensations now move on down into the base of your spine, your root chakra. Imagine a warmth in your root chakra as if a ray of sunlight were coming into the room and falling upon your spine . . . and it feels good. You imagine this warmth now moving up your spine . . . up your spine . . . up your spine and into the back of your neck and shoulder muscles. And your shoulder muscles are now loose and limp . . . loose and limp . . . just completely relaxed. And the relaxing sensations now move on up the back of your neck and into your scalp. Relaxing your scalp. Feel your scalp relaxing, and feel the relaxing sensations now drain down into your facial muscles, relaxing your facial muscles. Your jaw is relaxed. Allow a little space between your teeth. And your throat is relaxed. Your entire body is now relaxed all over in every way. And all tension is gone from your body and mind.

And we're now going to balance and energize your aura and attune you to the subtle vibrations that support the perception of subjective awareness. So to begin, imagine a beam of iridescent white light coming down from above and entering your crown chakra of spirituality on the top of your head. Imagine the light . . . create it with the unlimited power of your mind. This is the Universal light of life energy, and you feel it stimulating this chakra center, which is purple in color. Visualize a swirling vortex of purple, and the light opens, balances, and charges this chakra center. Imagine the opening, balancing, charging.

(Pause for five seconds.)

And the light is now moving on down into the center of your forehead—your brow chakra, which is a swirling blue-violet vortex of energy. Perceive the blue-violet color, and feel the balancing and energizing that is taking place here.

Opening, balancing, energizing.

(Pause for five seconds.)

And the light is now moving on down into your throat chakra, which is a swirling silvery-blue vortex of energy. Perceive the silvery-blue color, and feel the balancing and energizing that is taking place here. Opening, balancing, energizing.

(Pause for five seconds.)

And the light is now moving on down into your heart chakra, which is to be perceived as a golden glow. Perceive the golden color, and feel the balancing and energizing of your heart chakra center. Opening, balancing, energizing.

(Pause for five seconds.)

And the light is now moving on down into your solar plexus chakra, located at the level of your navel. This chakra is to be visualized as several shades of red in color. Perceive the red colors, and imagine the balancing and energizing that is taking place here. Opening, balancing, energizing.

(Pause for five seconds.)

And the light is moving on down into your sacral or spleen chakra, which is located a little below your navel. This swirling vortex of energy is a rainbow of colors. Perceive the many colors, and feel the balancing and energizing that is taking place here. Opening, balancing, energizing.

(Pause for five seconds.)

And the light is now moving on down into your root chakra at the base of your spine. This chakra is to be visualized as a swirling vortex of energy, red and orange in color. Perceive the reds and oranges, and feel the balancing and energizing that is taking place here. Opening, balancing, energizing.

(Pause for five seconds.)

And your chakras are opened, balanced, and charged, thus expanding your aura and attuning you to the subtle vibrations that support the perception of subjective awareness.

And it's now time to imagine the bright white light moving back up into heart area. Visualize your heart center overflowing with the Universal light of life energy.

And now imagine the light emerging from your heart center to surround your body in a protective aura of bright white God light.

And you are totally protected. Totally protected. Only your own Guides and Masters or highly evolved and loving entities who mean you well will be able to influence you in any way in this altered state of consciousness session.

And as you continue to focus upon the sound of my voice, I am going to count you down, down, down . . . so vividly imagine yourself in a situation going down . . . walking down stairs, downhill, down the side of a pyramid . . . or any situation in which you see yourself going down, while I count backwards from seven to one.

Number seven, deeper, deeper, deeper, down, down, down.

Number six, deeper, deeper, deeper, down, down, down.

Number five, deeper, deeper, deeper, down, down, down.

Number four, deeper, deeper, deeper, down, down, down.

Number three, deeper, deeper, deeper, down, down, down.

Number two, deeper, deeper, deeper, down, down, down. Number one, deeper, deeper, deeper, down, down, down.

And you're relaxed and at ease, and you feel deep. But let's go down a little deeper now . . . deeper now.

Number seven, deeper, deeper, deeper, down, down, down.

Number six, deeper, deeper, deeper, down, down, down.

Number five, deeper, deeper, deeper, down, down, down. Number four, deeper, deeper, deeper, down, down, down. Number three, deeper, deeper, deeper, down, down, down.

Number two, deeper, deeper, deeper, down, down, down. Number one, deeper, deeper, deeper, down, down, down.

And you are now relaxed and at ease, and a quietness of spirit permeates your body and mind. And it's time to go way back in time to a period in Spirit when you were planning your current life.

All right, it's time to imagine a tunnel with your inner eyes. This is a tunnel through time and space . . . and it can be any kind of tunnel that is pleasing to you. So vividly imagine the tunnel . . . and perceive yourself stepping into the tunnel and beginning to transfer in time and space as I count from five to one. On the count of one, you will step out of the end of the tunnel and find yourself back in Spirit during the time you were planning out your current life.

So, number five, you're in the tunnel and beginning to move through time and space. Allow it to happen. Feel it happening. You're just letting go and moving through the tunnel now . . . moving toward that light way down at the end.

Number four, moving through the tunnel to activate past memories . . . transcending time and space to better understand your totality.

Number three, moving through the tunnel to explore your rebirth planning session . . . and you're getting closer and closer to the light at the end.

Number two, you're almost there . . . almost there. On the next count, you will step out of the end of the tunnel and perceive yourself in Spirit, planning your current life.

And number one . . . you're now there.

Step out of the tunnel, and allow impressions to begin to form. You've returned to a time in Spirit when you were preparing to incarnate into your current life. So go ahead and perceive the environment very, very vividly. Are you outdoors or indoors? Vividly perceive your environment.

(Pause for forty-five seconds.)

Are you alone, or is there someone else there with you?

(Pause for twenty seconds.)

Maybe the soul who will be your Spirit Guide in the forthcoming incarnation is there with you. Maybe your Master teachers are nearby. If not, and if you can call them in, go ahead and do so now.

(Pause for thirty seconds.)

If others are present, perceive what they look like and how they're attired.

(Pause for thirty seconds.)

You've returned to a time in which you were planning a lifetime. So go ahead and explore how this works . . . what are you doing? What is happening?

(Pause for forty-five seconds.)

All right, I'd like you to explore some of your key decisions. First, let's look at what you've worked out in regard to primary relationships or lack of relationships in your life. Explore the different people you'll be getting together with.

(Pause for forty-five seconds.)

OK . . . now explore the primary lessons you hope to accomplish with these key people.

(Pause for sixty seconds.)

All right, remember everything you're perceiving, but it's time to explore your karmic directions. You've incarnated to explore a particular career or avocation. Or you may be planning more than one career. What are you planning as you do this soul mapping?

(Pause for forty-five seconds.)

All right, go ahead and explore other aspects of your Prebirth Planning session. Explore your choice of parents. Why have you picked the parents you decided upon? And what lessons do you hope to learn as a result of your parental choice?

(Pause for sixty seconds.)

All right, let's explore another aspect of your Prebirth Planning session. This time it's in regard to any children whom you destine to come through you . . . or maybe you'll parent other children through a marriage . . . or maybe you will decide not to have children in this life. Go ahead and explore the lessons you hope to learn through children or lack of children in your lifetime. Explore the plan and the relationships.

(Pause for sixty seconds.)

OK, now the next question is in regard to any soul contracts you are making. Are you agreeing to come together with other souls? Explore this in detail.

(Pause for sixty seconds.)

All right . . . if you do make soul contracts, do they have a termination date, or is the contract dependent upon how things work out between you? Explore this in detail.

(Pause for sixty seconds.)

OK . . . it's time for you to explore any soul contracts you've made with yourself. Also, be open to anything that comes in regarding free will related to promises you've made to yourself.

(Pause for sixty seconds.)

All right, let's move to the time you've completed your rebirth plans and are obtaining advice from the elders or Masters. Is there any disagreement about the way you've set it up? Perceive everything of importance that relates to your plan.

(Pause for sixty seconds.)

OK, let go of this now, and on the count of three, you'll be back in the present, remembering everything you've just experienced. On the count of three, you'll be back in the present, remaining with your eyes closed in a deep and peaceful altered state of consciousness. Number one . . . number two . . . and number three.

You're now back in the present, and in just a moment I'm going to count you up into Higher Self. At this level, you'll have at your mental fingertips full awareness of your totality, and you'll quickly and easily perceive all you desire to know about your life plan.

It's now time to move on up into your Higher Mind, your Higher Self. I'll count from one to eight, and as I do, vividly imagine yourself ascending up a beautiful stairway . . . higher and higher, ascending from your current level of awareness into Higher Mind. And on the count of eight, you'll be there.

So let go and imagine yourself ascending the stairs. Use your imagination very, very vividly.

Number one, you're letting go and ascending. Letting go and ascending, ascending, ascending . . . transcending levels of consciousness.

Number two, ascending, ascending, you're moving higher and higher.

Number three, ascending, ascending. You feel your leg muscles as you take each step going higher and higher.

Number four, ascending, ascending.

Number five, moving higher and higher and higher, up into your highest level of mind.

Number six, higher, higher.

Number seven, ascending, ascending, you're almost there.

And number eight, you're now there.

You now have access to your soul history and the collective unconscious. The secret to obtaining the wisdom is simply self-trust. Let's call in your Spirit Guide and ask for assistance. Call out silently in your mind and ask your Guide to join you. Hear your voice echo out across the Universe and back to you.

And it's time to call in your Spirit Guide and ask for assistance. Call out silently in your mind and ask your Guide to join us. Hear your voice echo out across the Universe and back to you.

(Pause for twenty seconds.)

And your Guide is now there with you. You may or may not perceive them visually, but if you desire to do so, simply trust the impressions that come into your mind. Are they appearing as male or female . . . young or old . . . and how are they dressed? *Trust your impressions.*

(Pause for thirty seconds.)

And you have the power and ability to communicate directly with your Guide using thought language. Ask questions with a thought, and then listen as the answer comes back to you in the form of another thought. And it's time to explore your rebirth plan in relationship to the way your life is unfolding. How is it all working out? Ask your guide.

(Pause for sixty seconds.)

Are there any changes you need to make? Listen to your Spirit Guide or Master teachers . . . or ask them questions with thought language. This is important. Learn about what you need to do to fulfill your life plan. What changes do you need to make?

(Pause for ninety seconds.)

All right, it is time to say goodbye to your Spirit Guide, knowing you have the power and ability to return and continue exploring at any time you desire to do so. So say your goodbyes.

(Pause for fifteen seconds.)

And in just a moment I'm going to wake you up. On the count of five, you will open your eyes and be wide awake, fully alert, thinking and acting with calm self-assurance. You'll awaken feeling as if you've just taken a relaxing nap, and you'll be at peace with yourself, the world, and everyone in it.

Number one, coming on up now and feeling an expanding spiritual light within.

Number two, coming up feeling at peace with all life.

Number three, coming on up and tapping into an internal balance and harmony.

Number four, recall the situation in the room.

And number five, wide awake, wide awake. Open your eyes and feel good. Number five, wide awake.

Resolve a Problem Meditation

This meditation is taken directly from an old file I found among my husband's papers. My guess is this was an old process he used in his Bushido Training.

Now that you have all this wisdom fresh in your mind, let's apply it to one particular situation in your life. I'd like you to think about your primary problem, other than a health problem. Your primary problem as it relates to others, your career, financial status, et cetera . . . and I'd like you to explore this situation in an altered state of consciousness.

So before we begin, pick a problem in your life you'd like to explore.

(Pause for ten seconds.)

You're breathing deeply and relaxing completely.

Breathing deeply and relaxing completely . . . and allowing a quietness of spirit to come in. Taking a deep breath in and holding it as long as you comfortably can . . . then let the breath out slowly through slightly parted lips, and when the breath is all the way out, push it further out, and further out . . . and then repeat the process. Breathing deeply, and when any outside thoughts come into your mind, simply brush them aside and tell yourself, "I'll deal with that later," and then return your concentration to the sound of my voice, and breathing deeply and relaxing completely.

And in just a moment I'm going to relax your body one part at a time. So play the role, play the part, and feel your body relaxing as I ask you to do so. And the relaxing power is coming into the toes of both of your feet at the same time . . . and it's moving right on down into the balls of your feet, into your arches, into your heels, and right on up to your ankles. Completely relaxed, completely relaxed . . . and the relaxing sensations now move on up your legs to your knees, relaxing all the muscles as it goes. And on up your legs now, to your thighs and to your hips. Permeating every cell and every atom.

And you're relaxing completely, relaxing completely, keeping your full attention on the sound of my voice and relaxing your body, as the relaxing sensations move on down into the fingers of both of your hands . . . relaxing your hands. Feel your hands relaxing. And your lower arms are relaxed, and your upper arms are relaxed. Fingers and hands and lower arms and upper arms . . . just completely relaxed.

And the relaxing sensations now move on down into the base of your spine, your root chakra. Imagine a warmth in your root chakra as if a ray of sunlight were coming into the room and falling upon your spine . . . and it feels good. You imagine this warmth now moving up your spine . . . up your spine . . . up your spine and into the back of your neck and shoulder muscles. And your shoulder muscles are now loose and limp . . . loose and limp . . . just completely relaxed. And the relaxing sensations now move on up the back of your neck and into your scalp. Relaxing your scalp.

Feel your scalp relaxing and feel the relaxing sensations now drain down into your facial muscles, relaxing your facial muscles. Your jaw is relaxed. Allow a little space between your teeth. And your throat is relaxed. Your entire body is now relaxed all over in every way. And all tension is gone from your body and mind.

And we're now going to balance and energize your aura and attune you to the subtle vibrations that support the perception of subjective awareness. So to begin, imagine a beam of iridescent white light coming down from above and entering your crown chakra of spirituality on the top of your head. Imagine the light . . . create it with the unlimited power of your mind. This is the Universal light of life energy, and you feel it stimulating this chakra center, which is purple in color. Visualize a swirling vortex of purple, and the light opens, balances, and charges this chakra center. Imagine the opening, balancing, charging.

(Pause for five seconds.)

And the light is now moving on down into the center of your forehead—your brow chakra, which is a swirling blue-violet vortex of energy. Perceive the blue-violet color, and feel the balancing and energizing that is taking place here.

Opening, balancing, energizing.

(Pause for five seconds.)

And the light is now moving on down into your throat chakra, which is a swirling silvery-blue vortex of energy.

Perceive the silvery-blue color, and feel the balancing and energizing that is taking place here. Opening, balancing, energizing.

(Pause for five seconds.)

And the light is now moving on down into your heart chakra, which is to be perceived as a golden glow. Perceive the golden color, and feel the balancing and energizing of your heart chakra center. Opening, balancing, energizing.

(Pause for five seconds.)

And the light is now moving on down into your solar plexus chakra, located at the level of your navel. This chakra is to be visualized as several shades of red in color. Perceive the red colors, and imagine the balancing and energizing that is taking place here. Opening, balancing, energizing.

(Pause for five seconds.)

And the light is moving on down into your sacral or spleen chakra, which is alocated a little below your navel. This swirling vortex of energy is a rainbow of colors. Perceive the many colors and feel the balancing and energizing that is taking place here. Opening, balancing, energizing.

(Pause for five seconds.)

And the light is now moving on down into your root chakra at the base of your spine. This chakra is to be visualized as a swirling vortex of energy, red and orange in color. Perceive the reds and oranges, and feel the balancing and energizing that is taking place here. Opening, balancing, energizing.

(Pause for five seconds.)

And your chakras are opened, balanced, and charged, thus expanding your aura and attuning you to the subtle vibrations that support the perception of subjective awareness.

And it's now time to imagine the bright white light moving back up into heart area. Visualize your heart center overflowing with the Universal light of life energy.

And now imagine the light emerging from your heart center to surround your body in a protective aura of bright white God light.

And you are totally protected. Totally protected. Only your own Guides and Masters or highly evolved and loving entities who mean you well will be able to influence you in any way in this altered state of consciousness session.

And as you continue to focus upon the sound of my voice, I am going to count you down, down, down . . . so vividly imagine yourself in a situation going down . . . walking down stairs, downhill, down the side of a pyramid . . . or any situation in which you see yourself going down, while I count backwards from seven to one.

Number seven, deeper, deeper, deeper, down, down, down.

Number six, deeper, deeper, deeper, down, down, down.

Number five, deeper, deeper, deeper, down, down, down.

Number four, deeper, deeper, deeper, down, down, down.

Number three, deeper, deeper, deeper, down, down, down.

Number two, deeper, deeper, deeper, down, down, down.

Number one, deeper, deeper, deeper, down, down, down.

And you're relaxed and at ease, and you feel deep. But let's go down a little deeper now . . . deeper now.

Number seven, deeper, deeper, deeper, down, down, down.

Number six, deeper, deeper, deeper, down, down, down.

Number five, deeper, deeper, deeper, down, down, down.

Number four, deeper, deeper, deeper, down, down, down.

Number three, deeper, deeper, deeper, down, down, down.

Number two, deeper, deeper, deeper, down, down, down. Number one, deeper, deeper, deeper, down, down, down.

And you are now relaxed and at ease, feeling at peace with yourself, the world, and everyone in it. All right, you have a problem you'd like to explore . . . you've picked a problem in your life, and I'd like you to clearly define it now, silently in your mind.

(Pause for ten seconds.)

All right, now . . . can you accept that on a karmic level you are responsible for your problem, yes or no?

(Pause for ten seconds.)

Have you acknowledged the problem as a reality as opposed to denying its existence, yes or no?

(Pause for ten seconds.)

Is there any kind of payoff in keeping the problem? By that I mean, are you somehow served in other ways by allowing the problem to continue, yes or no?

(Pause for ten seconds.)

Do you really desire to resolve this problem, yes or no?

(Pause for ten seconds.)

If another person is part of the problem, can you reframe the situation? Don't look at it as a conflict between competing solutions; instead, define it in terms of conflicting needs. What are your needs? What are the other person's needs?

(Pause for ninety seconds.)

The only way to really solve a problem involving others is to make it a win-win situation. Be creative . . . how can both of your needs be satisfied?

(Pause for ninety seconds.)

Are you assuming there are only a couple of solutions? If so, you're arguing for your limitations. There are probably numerous ways to achieve the results you desire. Ask yourself the right questions. Forget about what other people think, what society thinks. How else could you handle the situation?

(Pause for ninety seconds.)

Assuming you have various options to handle your problem, what are the prices and potential rewards of each option?

(Pause for ninety seconds.)

Are you willing to pay the price?

(Pause for twenty seconds.)

What do you really want to do? Not what is the best option, or the most realistic or sensible decision, but what do you really want to do?

(Pause for ninety seconds.)

What does that communicate to you?

(Pause for ten seconds.)

You are creating your own reality, your own future karma with every thought that flows through your mind. Everything you think, say, and do creates karma . . . and that includes the motive, intent, and desire behind everything you think, say, and do. So . . . what are you going to do?

(Pause for ninety seconds.)

All right, now for just a moment before awakening, visualize the situation as resolved. Very, very vividly in your mind, perceive the situation as resolved, and experience how you feel about it.

And in just a moment I'm going to wake you up. On the count of five, you will open your eyes and be wide awake, fully alert, thinking, and acting with calm self-assurance. You'll awaken feeling as if you've just taken a relaxing nap, and you'll be at peace with yourself, the world, and everyone in it.

Number one, coming on up now and feeling an expanding spiritual light within.

Number two, coming up feeling at peace with all life.

Number three, coming on up and tapping into an internal balance and harmony.

Number four, recall the situation in the room.

And number five, wide awake, wide awake. Open your eyes and feel good. Number five, wide awake.

Soul Fragments and Retrieval

Working with soul fragments is a powerful therapy technique to combine with hypnotherapy to help those who have experienced a loss—especially young children who have been sexually abused. Here's an example Dick gave to his students:

I was working with a sixteen-year-old girl who was starting to recall repressed memories of childhood molestation. She could not recall who did it to her. She didn't really want her mother to hear what she remembered. But she also wanted mom nearby. This was resolved with her mom agreeing to sit right outside my office with the door opened a few inches. The sixteen-year-old, whom I'll call Jan, was deep in hypnosis. I had taken her into past-life regression to see if the memories of molestation might be coming from another incarnation. They were not. So I was in the process of moving her up into Higher Self, into an all-knowing level of mind where, I explained, she could access her soul history.

As I had Jan climbing the stairs, she was about halfway up and had just reached a landing when she said, "Oh my, there I am at about the age of five." She was seeing her younger self on the stairs, indicating that a soul fragment of the five-year-old had broken off.

Like anyone experienced at doing soul fragments work, I knew Jan was calling out to me for help. I instructed her to go back to the cause of the original wounding in her current lifetime. She moved to a time her father was beginning to sexually molest her. She began to cry and then to scream. Obviously they were alone in the house.

"No pain, Jan. On the count of three the pain will be gone. One, two, three. You feel fine, and I'm removing the memories as well. On the count of three, the memories will just go away. One, the memories are just blowing away. Two, the memories are just floating away, and three, the memories are gone. All gone. How do you feel, Jan?"

"Fine," she said.

"What do you see, and what are you doing?" I asked.

"I'm just floating around," she said.

I awakened Jan and invited her mother back into the room. Jan had no conscious memory of her father molesting her. A soul fragment of the five-year-old had broken off and sought to hide every time her father approached her for sex over the last eleven years.

After talking with Jan about what had happened, she decided she didn't want to see or relive the experience with her father at age five. We all have a silver cord that connects our body to our soul. Even when a fragment of your soul breaks off to seek shelter elsewhere, it remains attached to your soul by fibers—silver threads of the cord. So all you do to find your missing fragment is to follow the threads into the spiritual dimensions until you reach this part of your totality.

So I hypnotized Jan again and asked her to perceive her silver cord and follow the threads. I also asked her Spirit

Guide or Guardian Angel to accompany her on this search. "When you find your mission soul fragment, speak up and tell me what's happening," I said.

After about ten minutes of silence, Jan spoke up, and claimed to have found her fragment. I said, "It's time to communicate with your soul fragment, Jan. Express your sincere desire to have it rejoin the whole. Address all of its concerns. Find out what would have to happen for it to feel secure enough to return."

After five more minutes of silence, Jan said, "My fragment is willing to rejoin my soul."

There were still many issues to be dealt with, including the mother wanting a divorce, legal custody of Jan, a restraining order barring the father from being alone with his daughter, and therapy for Jan. Most of these are out of a hypnotherapist's realm of expertise.

Soul Retrieval

Everyone trusted Dick Sutphen, but taking a client back to this type of trauma should only be done by a licensed, well-experienced hypnotherapist. This session is not to be done by anyone who is not a professional. The hypnotherapist is responsible for the client's well-being. Unless you know what you are doing, leave this type of work to the professionals.

You're breathing deeply and relaxing completely.

Breathing deeply and relaxing completely . . . and allowing a quietness of spirit to come in. Taking a deep breath in and holding it as long as you comfortably can . . . then let the breath out slowly through slightly parted lips, and when the breath is all the way out, push it further out, and further out . . . and then repeat the process. Breathing deeply, and when any outside thoughts come into your mind, simply brush them aside and tell yourself, "I'll deal with that later," and then return your concentration to the sound of my voice, and breathing deeply and relaxing completely.

And in just a moment, I'm going to relax your body one part at a time. So play the role, play the part, and feel your body relaxing as I ask you to do so. And the relaxing power is coming into the toes of both of your feet at the same time . . . and it's moving right on down into the balls of your feet, into your arches, into your heels, and right on up to your ankles. Completely relaxed, completely relaxed . . . and the relaxing sensations now move on up your legs to your knees, relaxing all the muscles as it goes. And on up your legs now, to your thighs and to your hips. Permeating every cell and every atom.

And you're relaxing completely, relaxing completely, keeping your full attention on the sound of my voice and relaxing your body, as the relaxing sensations move on down into the fingers of both of your hands . . . relaxing your hands. Feel your hands relaxing. And your lower arms are relaxed, and your upper arms are relaxed. Fingers and hands and lower arms and upper arms . . . just completely relaxed.

And the relaxing sensations now move on down into the base of your spine, your root chakra. Imagine a warmth in your root chakra as if a ray of sunlight were coming into the room and falling upon your spine . . . and it feels good. You imagine this warmth now moving up your spine . . . up your spine . . . up your spine and into the back of your

neck and shoulder muscles. And your shoulder muscles are now loose and limp . . . loose and limp . . . just completely relaxed. And the relaxing sensations now move on up the back of your neck and into your scalp. Relaxing your scalp. Feel your scalp relaxing, and feel the relaxing sensations now drain down into your facial muscles, relaxing your facial muscles. Your jaw is relaxed. Allow a little space between your teeth. And your throat is relaxed. Your entire body is now relaxed all over in every way. And all tension is gone from your body and mind.

And we're now going to balance and energize your aura and attune you to the subtle vibrations that support the perception of subjective awareness. So to begin, imagine a beam of iridescent white light coming down from above and entering your crown chakra of spirituality on the top of your head. Imagine the light . . . create it with the unlimited power of your mind. This is the Universal light of life energy, and you feel it stimulating this chakra center, which is purple in color. Visualize a swirling vortex of purple, and the light opens, balances, and charges this chakra center. Imagine the opening, balancing, charging.

(Pause for five seconds.)

And the light is now moving on down into the center of your forehead—your brow chakra, which is a swirling blue-violet vortex of energy. Perceive the blue-violet color, and feel the balancing and energizing that is taking place here. Opening, balancing, energizing.

(Pause for five seconds.)

And the light is now moving on down into your throat chakra, which is a swirling silvery-blue vortex of energy.

Perceive the silvery-blue color, and feel the balancing and energizing that is taking place here. Opening, balancing, energizing.

(Pause for five seconds.)

And the light is now moving on down into your heart chakra, which is to be perceived as a golden glow. Perceive the golden color, and feel the balancing and energizing of your heart chakra center. Opening, balancing, energizing.

(Pause for five seconds.)

And the light is now moving on down into your solar plexus chakra, located at the level of your navel. This chakra is to be visualized as several shades of red in color. Perceive the red colors, and imagine the balancing and energizing that is taking place here. Opening, balancing, energizing.

(Pause for five seconds.)

And the light is moving on down into your sacral or spleen chakra, which is located a little below your navel. This swirling vortex of energy is a rainbow of colors. Perceive the many colors, and feel the balancing and energizing that is taking place here. Opening, balancing, energizing.

(Pause for five seconds.)

And the light is now moving on down into your root chakra at the base of your spine. This chakra is to be visualized as a swirling vortex of energy, red and orange in color. Perceive the reds and oranges, and feel the balancing and energizing that is taking place here. Opening, balancing, energizing.

(Pause for five seconds.)

And your chakras are opened, balanced, and charged, thus expanding your aura and attuning you to the subtle vibrations that support the perception of subjective awareness.

And it's now time to imagine the bright white light moving back up into heart area. Visualize your heart center overflowing with the Universal light of life energy.

And now imagine the light emerging from your heart center to surround your body in a protective aura of bright white God light.

And you are totally protected. Totally protected. Only your own Guides and Masters or highly evolved and loving entities who mean you well will be able to influence you in any way in this altered state of consciousness session.

It's now time to move on up into your Higher Mind, your Higher Self. And at this level you'll have at your mental fingertips access to all knowledge of all the lifetimes you've ever lived . . . if you'll only trust what you perceive . . . I'll count from one to eight, and as I do, vividly imagine yourself ascending up a beautiful stairway . . . higher and higher, ascending from your current level of awareness into Higher Mind. And on the count of eight you'll be there.

So let go and imagine yourself ascending the stairs. Use your imagination very, very vividly.

Number one, you're letting go and ascending. Letting go and ascending, ascending, ascending . . . transcending levels of consciousness.

Number two, ascending, ascending, you're moving higher and higher.

Number three, ascending, ascending. You feel your leg muscles as you take each step, going higher and higher.

Number four, ascending, ascending.

Number five, moving higher and higher and higher, up into your highest level of mind.

Number six, higher, higher.

Number seven, ascending, ascending, you're almost there.

And number eight, you're now there.

You now have access to your soul history and the collective unconscious. The secret to obtaining the wisdom is simply self-trust . . . And let's call in your Spirit Guide and ask for assistance. Call out silently in your mind and ask your Guide to join you. Hear your voice echo out across the Universe and back to you.

(Pause for ten seconds.)

Those who love, teach, and guide you are now here to assist us in obtaining awareness. And I'd like you to begin this exploration by looking back over your life. Can you recall any traumas that may have resulted in soul loss? Think back, and know that those in Spirit may be helping you to remember.

Be aware of all thoughts, feelings, or visualizations. When you locate something, speak up and tell me.

(Pause for five seconds.)

All right, remember all you're perceiving, but it's now time for you to use your inner eyes to scan your body in search for any missing fragments. And I'm asking those who love, teach, and guide you in Spirit to assist. Watch for any shadowy areas or empty places. If you find anything, speak up and let me know.

(Pause for five seconds.)

If you are noting traumas or what appears to be missing portions of your totality, remember them. But it is now time to regress back in time to the original wounding. If you have suffered more than one trauma, you will now explore the primary missing fragment. So imagine yourself in a tunnel leading back into your past. I will count from five to one as you move through the tunnel . . . back in time . . . back to the event that caused your soul loss.

Number five, you're letting go and beginning to move back in time. Allow it to happen. Feel it happening. See yourself moving through the tunnel back into the past.

Number four, moving back to the event that caused your soul loss.

Number three, you're moving through the tunnel toward a light way down at the end.

Number two, on the next count you will step out of the end of the tunnel and you will perceive, without pain or emotion, what happened to cause your soul loss.

Number one, you're now there.

Step out of the tunnel, and allow the impressions to begin to come in. . . . are you outdoors or indoors?

(Begin questioning what happened and when it happened as you would in a past-life regression. Keep in mind, your client may be in the present life or a past life. Once you have discovered everything you can about the situation, bring your client back into Higher Self, where the spirit helpers await.)

On the count of three, you'll be back in the present, remembering everything you just experienced.

(If your client is resistant to what they just experienced, you may have to regress them back to what they did in a prior incarnation that set this conflict into play.

Once they accept that they acted in a way that generated a reaction, they will be more likely to accept the justice of the situation. Upon returning to Higher Self, you will want to obtain a karmic overview of the situation. If the soul loss took place in a past life, you will want to find out if any of those who played a role in the soul loss are playing roles in your client's life today. We tend to reincarnate over and over with the same people until we resolve our issues.)

All right, it's now time to seek out your missing soul fragment. We all have a silver cord that connects our body to our soul . . . and even when a fragment of your soul breaks off to seek shelter elsewhere, it remains attached to your soul by fibers—silver threads of the cord. So all you have to do to find your missing fragment is to follow the threads into the spiritual dimensions until you reach this part of your totality.

(Pause for five seconds.)

So go ahead now. Perceive your silver cord . . . and if you look closely, you'll notice that there are fibrous silver threads leading away from your main cord . . . and it's time to begin following the threads. Those who love, teach, and guide you will accompany you on this search. When you find your missing soul fragment, speak up and tell me what is happening.

(When the client speaks up, respond appropriately.)

It is now time to communicate with your fragment. Express your sincere desire to have it rejoin the whole. Address all of its concerns. Find out what would have to happen for it to feel secure enough to return.

(As the hypnotherapist, you will most likely get involved in the dialogue, helping to provide assurances to the fragment.)

If the fragment is willing to rejoin your soul, embrace each other and allow this merger to take place.

(Guide this process, which can be lengthy and emotional.)

And it is now time to return to Higher Self with your fragment having rejoined your soul. On the count of three, you'll be back in Higher Self, feeling relaxed and at ease, and fully integrated for the first time in a long time. Number one, number two, number three.

(Once your client has recovered the soul fragment, they will want to nurture that part of themselves. If the fragment splintered off when your client was a child, the child won't immediately grow up. Explain this to your client. Dialogue with your client, who is still in trance. It will be time to do some intense forgiveness processing. To fully release the past, they will need to forgive themselves and all the others involved in the soul loss traumas. Provide a releasing mantra. Awaken your client with positive suggestions to the effect that they are fully integrated, etc. If there are several missing fragments, you'll have to deal with them one at a time, just as you would work with one past life at a time.)

And in just a moment I'm going to wake you up. On the count of five, you will open your eyes and be wide awake, fully alert, thinking and acting with calm self-assurance. You'll awaken feeling as if you've just taken a relaxing nap, and you'll be at peace with yourself, the world, and everyone in it.

Number one, coming on up now and feeling an expanding spiritual light within.

Number two, coming up feeling at peace with all life.

Number three, coming on up and tapping into an internal balance and harmony.

Number four, recall the situation in the room.

And number five, wide awake, wide awake. Open your eyes and feel good. Number five, wide awake.

Soul Group Regression

Soul Groups are sets of individuals who share similarities, such as goals, desires and vibrational rates. Each Soul Group is different. Some have only a few individuals, while others may consist of hundreds of souls. They tend to reincarnate together to experience lifetimes from which they will all benefit. Your current family and close friends could be a part of your Soul Group, switching roles during different lifetimes. Or your Soul Group may choose not to be born in the same family unit. Members may live separate lives in different areas where they will not meet, yet after the lives are completed, they will share their experiences with the rest of the group.

To do this process, you will need to discuss the concepts of Soul Groups to familiarize your client or audience with what they are. Richard and I conducted hundreds of these at different seminars over a ten-year period, and everyone in the audience went to some type of garden. They always met with their loved ones and oftentimes with their Spirit Guides and Masters.

You're breathing deeply and relaxing completely.

Breathing deeply and relaxing completely ... and allowing a quietness of spirit to come in. Taking a deep breath in and holding it as long as you comfortably can ... then let the breath out slowly through slightly parted lips, and when the breath is all the way out, push it further out, and further out . . . and then repeat the process. Breathing deeply, and when any outside thoughts come into your mind, simply brush them aside and tell yourself, "I'll deal with that later," and then return your concentration to the sound of my voice, and breathing deeply and relaxing completely.

And in just a moment I'm going to relax your body one part at a time. So play the role, play the part, and feel your body relaxing as I ask you to do so. And the relaxing power is coming into the toes of both of your feet at the same time . . . and it's moving right on down into the balls of your feet, into your arches, into your heels, and right on up to your ankles. Completely relaxed, completely relaxed . . . and the relaxing sensations now move on up your legs to your knees, relaxing all the muscles as it goes. And on up your legs now, to your thighs and to your hips. Permeating every cell and every atom.

And you're relaxing completely, relaxing completely, keeping your full attention on the sound of my voice and relaxing your body, as the relaxing sensations move on down into the fingers of both of your hands . . . relaxing your hands. Feel your hands relaxing. And your lower arms are relaxed, and your upper arms are relaxed. Fingers and hands and lower arms and upper arms . . . just completely relaxed.

And the relaxing sensations now move on down into the base of your spine, your root chakra. Imagine a warmth in your root chakra as if a ray of sunlight were coming into the room and falling upon your spine . . . and it feels good.

You imagine this warmth now moving up your spine . . . up your spine . . . up your spine and into the back of your neck and shoulder muscles. And your shoulder muscles are now loose and limp . . . loose and limp . . . just completely relaxed. And the relaxing sensations now move on up the back of your neck and into your scalp. Relaxing your scalp. Feel your scalp relaxing, and feel the relaxing sensations now drain down into your facial muscles, relaxing your facial muscles. Your jaw is relaxed. Allow a little space between your teeth. And your throat is relaxed. Your entire body is now relaxed all over in every way. And all tension is gone from your body and mind.

And we're now going to balance and energize your aura and attune you to the subtle vibrations that support the perception of subjective awareness. So to begin, imagine a beam of iridescent white light coming down from above and entering your crown chakra of spirituality on the top of your head. Imagine the light . . . create it with the unlimited power of your mind. This is the Universal light of life energy, and you feel it stimulating this chakra center, which is purple in color. Visualize a swirling vortex of purple, and the light opens, balances, and charges this chakra center. Imagine the opening, balancing, charging.

(Pause for five seconds.)

And the light is now moving on down into the center of your forehead—your brow chakra, which is a swirling blue-violet vortex of energy. Perceive the blue-violet color, and feel the balancing and energizing that is taking place here. Opening, balancing, energizing.

(Pause for five seconds.)

And the light is now moving on down into your throat chakra, which is a swirling silvery-blue vortex of energy.

Perceive the silvery-blue color, and feel the balancing and energizing that is taking place here. Opening, balancing, energizing.

(Pause for five seconds.)

And the light is now moving on down into your heart chakra, which is to be perceived as a golden glow. Perceive the golden color, and feel the balancing and energizing of your heart chakra center. Opening, balancing, energizing.

(Pause for five seconds.)

And the light is now moving on down into your solar plexus chakra, located at the level of your navel. This chakra is to be visualized as several shades of red in color. Perceive the red colors, and imagine the balancing and energizing that is taking place here. Opening, balancing, energizing.

(Pause for five seconds.)

And the light is moving on down into your sacral or spleen chakra, which is located a little below your navel. This swirling vortex of energy is a rainbow of colors. Perceive the many colors, and feel the balancing and energizing that is taking place here. Opening, balancing, energizing.

(Pause for five seconds.)

And the light is now moving on down into your root chakra at the base of your spine. This chakra is to be visualized as a swirling vortex of energy, red and orange in color. Perceive the reds and oranges, and feel the balancing and energizing that is taking place here. Opening, balancing, energizing.

(Pause for five seconds.)

And your chakras are opened, balanced, and charged, thus expanding your aura and attuning you to the subtle vibrations that support the perception of subjective awareness.

And it's now time to imagine the bright white light moving back up into heart area. Visualize your heart center overflowing with the Universal light of life energy.

And now imagine the light emerging from your heart center to surround your body in a protective aura of bright white God light.

And you are totally protected. Totally protected. Only your own Guides and Masters or highly evolved and loving entities who mean you well will be able to influence you in any way in this altered state of consciousness session.

And as you continue to focus upon the sound of my voice, I am going to count you down, down, down . . . so vividly imagine yourself in a situation going down . . . walking down stairs, downhill, down the side of a pyramid . . . or any situation in which you see yourself going down, while I count backwards from seven to one.

Number seven, deeper, deeper, deeper, down, down, down.

Number six, deeper, deeper, deeper, down, down, down.

Number five, deeper, deeper, deeper, down, down, down.

Number four, deeper, deeper, deeper, down, down, down.

Number three, deeper, deeper, deeper, down, down, down.

Number two, deeper, deeper, deeper, down, down, down. Number one, deeper, deeper, deeper, down, down, down.

And you're relaxed and at ease, and you feel deep. But let's go down a little deeper now . . . deeper now.

Number seven, deeper, deeper, deeper, down, down, down.

Number six, deeper, deeper, deeper, down, down, down.

Number five, deeper, deeper, deeper, down, down, down.

Number four, deeper, deeper, deeper, down, down, down.

Number three, deeper, deeper, deeper, down, down, down.

Number two, deeper, deeper, deeper, down, down, down. Number one, deeper, deeper, deeper, down, down, down.

And you are now completely relaxed and at ease. And if you feel uncomfortable at any time, you can easily bring yourself up by counting up from one to five and saying the words, "Wide awake."

And you're relaxed and at ease, and a quietness of spirit fills your body and mind. And you are about to move to a place in the spiritual realms where your Soul Group resides . . . So on the count of three, you'll perceive a park-like environment in the general area of your Soul Group . . . And you'll soon meet a member of your group who will guide you to the place where you meet.

So, on the count of three, perceive a beautiful garden. A garden where you may observe many people mingling . . .

Enjoying themselves. Be aware of the activity and the lightness you feel being here. Observe everything about this environment.

Number one, number two, and number three. New impressions.

(Pause for one minute.)

And if you have not already done so, in a few moments you will meet someone who seems very familiar to you. This person is a member of your Soul Group . . . And they will lead you to the place where you'll meet with other members of your group. On the count of three, new impressions. Number one, number two, and number three.

(Pause for one minute.)

And you follow this person to a place in spirit where you all meet . . . And on the count of three you'll be there. Number one, number two, and number three.

(Pause for one minute.)

You can communicate with others of your group, using thought language. Ask a question in thought, and receive your response with your next thought. Once developed, this technique is very effective. Do this now. Get to know the people of your Soul Group.

(Pause for two minutes.)

Observe what your group's meeting place is like. Is it within a building, is it a class room or is it outside?

(Pause for thirty seconds.)

Is your group large or small? How many souls are in your group?

(Pause for twenty seconds.)

Is your group leader there? If so, notice everything you can about your group leader.

(Pause for forty seconds.)

How often do you check in with your Soul Group?

(Pause for thirty seconds.)

What is your Soul Group's main purpose? Or what are you all working on?

(Pause for forty seconds.)

Is there anyone in your day-to-day life on earth at this time who is part of your Soul Group in Spirit?

(Pause for thirty seconds. Consider asking more questions, such as, "How many lives have you lived here on earth?" "How many more lives do you plan to live on earth?" "What is your real soul name?" "Do members of your group come and go, or do they graduate and move on to other more advanced Soul Groups?"

(Or use this opportunity to learn more about how reincarnation works, with questions such as: "Have you ever volunteered to live a life that would serve others, such as being someone most people hated, to give them the chance to learn about themselves?" "Have you ever incarnated to be a victim? What did you learn as a result, and what did others learn?" "Were you ever a perpetrator of human suffering?" "What did you do in the past that generated a great deal of karma you needed to balance?")

All right . . . it's time to let go of this and return to the present on the count of three. Your eyes will remain closed, and you'll continue to experience a peaceful altered state of consciousness, but on the count of three, you'll be back in the present, remembering everything you just experienced in the past.

Number one . . . number two . . . and number three.

And in just a moment I'm going to wake you up. On the count of five, you will open your eyes and be wide awake, fully alert, thinking and acting with calm self-assurance. You'll awaken feeling as if you've just taken a relaxing nap, and you'll be at peace with yourself, the world, and everyone in it.

Number one, coming on up now and feeling an expanding spiritual light within.

Number two, coming up feeling at peace with all life.

Number three, coming on up and tapping into an internal balance and harmony.

Number four, recall the situation in the room.

And number five, wide awake, wide awake. Open your eyes and feel good. Number five, wide awake.

Soul Mate Hypnosis Script

You're breathing deeply and relaxing completely.

Breathing deeply and relaxing completely . . . and allowing a quietness of spirit to come in. Taking a deep breath in and holding it as long as you comfortably can . . . then let the breath out slowly through slightly parted lips, and when the breath is all the way out, push it further out, and further out . . . and then repeat the process. Breathing deeply, and when any outside thoughts come into your mind, simply brush them aside and tell yourself, "I'll deal with that later," and then return your concentration to the sound of my voice, and breathing deeply and relaxing completely.

And in just a moment I'm going to relax your body one part at a time. So play the role, play the part, and feel your body relaxing as I ask you to do so. And the relaxing power is coming into the toes of both of your feet at the same time . . . and it's moving right on down into the balls of your feet, into your arches, into your heels, and right on up to your ankles. Completely relaxed, completely relaxed . . . and the relaxing sensations now move on up your legs to your knees, relaxing all the muscles as it goes. And on up your legs now, to your thighs and to your hips. Permeating every cell and every atom.

And you're relaxing completely, relaxing completely, keeping your full attention on the sound of my voice and relaxing your body, as the relaxing sensations move on down into the fingers of both of your hands . . . relaxing your hands. Feel your hands relaxing. And your lower arms are relaxed, and your upper arms are relaxed. Fingers and hands and lower arms and upper arms . . . just completely relaxed.

And the relaxing sensations now move on down into the base of your spine, your root chakra. Imagine a warmth in your root chakra, as if a ray of sunlight were coming into the room and falling upon your spine . . . and it feels good. You imagine this warmth now moving up your spine . . . up your spine . . . up your spine and into the back of your neck and shoulder muscles. And your shoulder muscles are now loose and limp . . . loose and limp . . . just completely relaxed. And the relaxing sensations now move on up the back of your neck and into your scalp. Relaxing your scalp. Feel your scalp relaxing, and feel the relaxing sensations now drain down into your facial muscles, relaxing your facial muscles. Your jaw is relaxed. Allow a little space between your teeth. And your throat is relaxed. Your entire body is now relaxed all over in every way. And all tension is gone from your body and mind.

And we're now going to balance and energize your aura and attune you to the subtle vibrations that support the perception of subjective awareness. So to begin, imagine a beam of iridescent white light coming down from above and entering your crown chakra of spirituality on the top

of your head. Imagine the light . . . create it with the unlimited power of your mind. This is the Universal light of life energy, and you feel it stimulating this chakra center, which is purple in color. Visualize a swirling vortex of purple, and the light opens, balances, and charges this chakra center. Imagine the opening, balancing, charging.

(Pause for five seconds.)

And the light is now moving on down into the center of your forehead—your brow chakra, which is a swirling blue-violet vortex of energy. Perceive the blue-violet color, and feel the balancing and energizing that is taking place here. Opening, balancing, energizing.

(Pause for five seconds.)

And the light is now moving on down into your throat chakra, which is a swirling silvery-blue vortex of energy.

Perceive the silvery-blue color, and feel the balancing and energizing that is taking place here. Opening, balancing, energizing.

(Pause for five seconds.)

And the light is now moving on down into your heart chakra, which is to be perceived as a golden glow. Perceive the golden color, and feel the balancing and energizing of your heart chakra center. Opening, balancing, energizing.

(Pause for five seconds.)

And the light is now moving on down into your solar plexus chakra, located at the level of your navel. This chakra is to be visualized as several shades of red in color. Perceive the red colors, and imagine the balancing and energizing that is taking place here. Opening, balancing, energizing.

(Pause for five seconds.)

And the light is moving on down into your sacral or spleen chakra, which is located a little below your navel. This swirling vortex of energy is a rainbow of colors. Perceive the many colors and feel the balancing and energizing that is taking place here. Opening, balancing, energizing.

(Pause for five seconds.)

And the light is now moving on down into your root chakra at the base of your spine. This chakra is to be visualized as a swirling vortex of energy, red and orange in color. Perceive the reds and oranges, and feel the balancing and energizing that is taking place here. Opening, balancing, energizing.

(Pause for five seconds.)

And your chakras are opened, balanced, and charged, thus expanding your aura and attuning you to the subtle vibrations that support the perception of subjective awareness.

And it's now time to imagine the bright white light moving back up into heart area. Visualize your heart center overflowing with the Universal light of life energy. And now imagine the light emerging from your heart center to surround your body in a protective aura of bright white God light.

And you are totally protected. Totally protected. Only your own Guides and Masters or highly evolved and loving entities who mean you well will be able to influence you in any way in this altered state of consciousness session.

And as you continue to focus upon the sound of my voice, I am going to count you down, down, down . . . so vividly imagine yourself in a situation going down . . . walking down stairs, downhill, down the side of a pyramid . . . or any situation in which you see yourself going down, while I count backwards from seven to one.

Number seven, deeper, deeper, deeper, down, down, down.

Number six, deeper, deeper, deeper, down, down, down.

Number five, deeper, deeper, deeper, down, down, down.

Number four, deeper, deeper, deeper, down, down, down. Number three, deeper, deeper, deeper, down, down, down.

Number two, deeper, deeper, deeper, down, down, down.

Number one, deeper, deeper, deeper, down, down, down.

And you're relaxed and at ease and you feel deep. But let's go down a little deeper now . . . deeper now.

Number seven, deeper, deeper, deeper, down, down, down.

Number six, deeper, deeper, deeper, down, down, down.

Number five, deeper, deeper, deeper, down, down, down.

Number four, deeper, deeper, deeper, down, down, down.

Number three, deeper, deeper, deeper, down, down, down.

Number two, deeper, deeper, deeper, down, down, down.

Number one, deeper, deeper, deeper, down, down, down.

And you are now relaxed and at ease, and you feel in balance and in harmony. A quietness of spirit permeates your body and mind... and you are open to awareness that will assist you to find and keep your soul mate.

You have beliefs about relationships that are the basis of your current reality. These beliefs generate the thoughts and emotions that create your relationship experiences, or lack of relationship experiences. To better explore some of your beliefs, I'm going to begin a sentence, and you will finish it instantly in your mind. Don't stop long enough to even think about it... just instantly, mentally, finish the sentence I begin. Then take a few moments to look at your emotions in regard to each response. Maybe you'll respond positively to a sentence... or maybe you'll respond negatively... any negative responses will indicate a belief area you need to work on.

OK... let's get started. Finish these sentences:

The idea of fully committing, mentally, emotionally, and financially, to a lover makes me feel...

When I think about opening up and trusting a new lover, I feel...

The idea of taking on the responsibility of a one-to-one relationship makes me feel...

Some people seem to avoid relationships because they fear the potential loss of their lover, or they fear abandonment. I think such a fear is...

OK, now remember how you've responded, because how you finished the sentences may reveal your deep-seated beliefs about these life areas. But now, I'd like to finish a few more sentences about relationships.

Here's the first one:

I believe my chance of finding and establishing a soul mate relationship is . . .

If I were in the soul mate relationship I desire, a lot of things in my life would change. The changes I wouldn't like are . . .

(Pause for ten seconds.)

All right . . . now these changes you don't like may be subconscious blocks that are keeping you from finding your soul mate. In other words, there may be a payoff in keeping things the way they are. Meditate on this for a few moments.

(Pause for one minute.)

OK, now trust the first thought that comes into your mind. Here's another sentence to finish:

The primary reason I haven't been able to find a soul mate is . . .

(Pause for five seconds.)

All right . . . now in regard to the way you finished the last sentence, did you blame others or outside circumstances in any way? If so, what if you were to accept the blame for not having the relationship you desire? If karma is the basis of reality, there is no one to blame for anything. You've created your current situation as a way of dealing with old fears you need to integrate. Assume for a minute that this is the case: you're to blame, and any change depends upon your actions. Consider this and how you could best respond.

(Pause for one minute.)

OK, here's another question:

Do you think that your beliefs about finding a soul mate are working against you? Yes or no?

(Pause for five seconds.)

If so, what belief is primarily working against you?

(Pause for five seconds.)

All right . . . hopefully you're aware of beliefs that are working against you . . . and these are fears you need to integrate to establish the soul mate relationship you desire. You can't change what you don't recognize, but in recognizing beliefs that don't work, you can face and embrace them. Courage is the willingness to be afraid and act anyway. Meditate upon this for a few moments.

(Pause for one minute.)

It's time to liberate yourself. It's time to do what works for you. It's time to improve the quality of your life, and to become all you are capable of being in all areas of your life . . . It's time to go out and get involved with people . . . to find the relationship you desire.

And now, before you awake, I'd like to take a few moments to vividly imagine what an ideal relationship would be like.

Create a mental movie in which you are writer, producer, director, and star. Vividly perceive yourself experiencing an ideal relationship. Do this now while I am quiet for a while.

(Pause for two minutes.)

And you have just seen your own reality. And in just a moment, I'm going to wake you up.

On the count of five, you will open your eyes and be wide awake, fully alert, thinking and acting with calm self-assurance. You'll awaken feeling as if you've just taken a relaxing nap, and you'll be at peace with yourself, the world, and everyone in it.

Number one, coming on up now and feeling an expanding spiritual light within.

Number two, coming up feeling at peace with all life.

Number three, coming on up and tapping into an internal balance and harmony.

Number four, recall the situation in the room.

And number five, wide awake, wide awake. Open your eyes and feel good. Number five, wide awake.

Spirit Guides

Dick encouraged his students and clients to develop a real work-ing relationship with the Guides, Masters, and loved ones who guide and protect you throughout your lifetime.

In 2010, Richard and I were at the annual National Guild of Hypnotists (NGH) meeting, waiting for Richard's turn to speak. I'd spent the day listening to several hypnotists discussing new concepts they were using in their practices and hearing the latest thoughts about giving sessions over the phone or Internet.

Richard's methods were very different from most of the speak-ers. Richard no longer gave straight hypnosis programming to his clients, and he only taught his students metaphysical or spir-itual hypnosis. I asked him why. He replied that programming will work, but one programming session would last no more than seven to ten days, on average. He found he could use his Spirit Contact therapy technique, in which he brought his clients back to the cause of their issue, and their issues could literally be solved in one session. He wasn't interested in repeat clients. In fact, he had so many people who wanted to see him that he found the only way to find answers for them quickly was to ask their Spirit Guides, Masters, and loved ones who had crossed over into Spirit to help them find solutions that always began in a prior lifetime.

The script in this chapter is to enable the client to make initial contact with their Spirit Guide. Past life regressions appear in the chapters "Chakra Link Meditation," "Soul Group Regression," and "Soul Retrieval."

Here are Dick's presession notes:

Before conducting a session, I usually talk with my client/ subject for about a half hour. I want to learn about many life issues or interests we can explore, because once the process is set into play, we will obtain a lot of information quickly. I also want to know if my client has a working relationship with a Spirit Guide or Guardian Angel, and if they do not, I tell them how we will set that up. I also ask if they have any deceased loved ones that they trusted in life—friends or relatives who are now in Spirit that they would like to join us. I also call in support guides and Master Teachers my client works with when out of body, on the other side, sleeping at night.

Begin the session by directing a full body relaxation, followed by chakra balancing and energizing and an intense protective ritual. Then do a double seven to one countdown. Provide an appropriate setup talk. At this point in a private session, you may want to count your client up into Higher Self, where they will meet those who love teach and guide them in spirit, and you then direct the exploration. Ask those in Spirit for answers, and quickly move your client in and out of the past to directly view earlier-life or past-life cause and effect. If the past drama is not too emotional or violent, have them relive the experience.

Another approach would be to start off with a past-life regression back to one of their key issues, or to the lifetime most influencing their current life. When that exploration is complete, bring them back to the present, remaining with their eyes closed in a deep altered state of consciousness. Next, count them up into Higher Self, and if they do not have a working relationship with their Spirit Guide or Angel, direct this meeting. Call in their deceased loved ones. (See script below.)

Meet Your Spirit Guide

You're breathing deeply and relaxing completely.

Breathing deeply and relaxing completely... and allowing a quietness of spirit to come in. Taking a deep breath in and holding it as long as you comfortably can ... then let the breath out slowly through slightly parted lips, and when the breath is all the way out, push it further out, and further out ... and then repeat the process. Breathing deeply, and when any outside thoughts come into your mind, simply brush them aside and tell yourself, "I'll deal with that later," and then return your concentration to the sound of my voice, and breathing deeply and relaxing completely.

And in just a moment I'm going to relax your body one part at a time. So play the role, play the part, and feel your body relaxing as I ask you to do so. And the relaxing power is coming into the toes of both of your feet at the same time ... and it's moving right on down into the balls of your feet, into your arches, into your heels, and right on up to your ankles. Completely relaxed, completely relaxed . . . and the relaxing sensation now moves on up your legs to your knees, relaxing all the muscles as it goes. And on up your legs now, to your thighs and to your hips. Permeating every cell and every atom.

And you're relaxing completely, relaxing completely, keeping your full attention on the sound of my voice and relaxing your body, as the relaxing sensations move on down into the fingers of both of your hands . . . relaxing your hands. Feel your hands relaxing. And your lower arms are relaxed, and your upper arms are relaxed. Fingers and hands and lower arms and upper arms . . . just completely relaxed.

And the relaxing sensations now move on down into the base of your spine, your root chakra. Imagine a warmth in your root chakra as if a ray of sunlight were coming into the room and falling upon your spine . . . and it feels good. You imagine this warmth now moving up your spine . . . up your spine . . . up your spine and into the back of your neck and shoulder muscles. And your shoulder muscles are now loose and limp . . . loose and limp . . . just completely relaxed.

And the relaxing sensations now move on up the back of your neck and into your scalp. Relaxing your scalp. Feel your scalp relaxing, and feel the relaxing sensations now drain down into your facial muscles, relaxing your facial muscles. Your jaw is relaxed. Allow a little space between your teeth. And your throat is relaxed. Your entire body is now relaxed all over in every way. And all tension is gone from your body and mind.

And we're now going to balance and energize your aura and attune you to the subtle vibrations that support the perception of subjective awareness. So to begin, imagine a beam of iridescent white light coming down from above and entering your crown chakra of spirituality on the top of your head. Imagine the light . . . create it with the unlimited power of your mind. This is the Universal light of life energy, and you feel it stimulating this chakra center, which is purple in color. Visualize a swirling vortex of purple, and the light opens, balances, and charges this chakra center. Imagine the opening, balancing, charging.

(Pause for five seconds.)

And the light is now moving on down into the center of your forehead—your brow chakra, which is a swirling blue-violet vortex of energy. Perceive the blue-violet color, and feel the balancing and energizing that is taking place here. Opening, balancing, energizing.

(Pause for five seconds.)

And the light is now moving on down into your throat chakra, which is a swirling silvery-blue vortex of energy.

Perceive the silvery-blue color, and feel the balancing and energizing that is taking place here. Opening, balancing, energizing.

(Pause for five seconds.)

And the light is now moving on down into your heart chakra, which is to be perceived as a golden glow. Perceive the golden color, and feel the balancing and energizing of your heart chakra center. Opening, balancing, energizing.

(Pause for five seconds.)

And the light is now moving on down into your solar plexus chakra, located at the level of your navel. This chakra is to be visualized as several shades of red in color. Perceive the red colors, and imagine the balancing and energizing that is taking place here. Opening, balancing, energizing.

(Pause for five seconds.)

And the light is moving on down into your sacral or spleen chakra, which is located a little below your navel. This swirling vortex of energy is a rainbow of colors. Perceive the many colors and feel the balancing and energizing that is taking place here. Opening, balancing, energizing.

(Pause for five seconds.)

And the light is now moving on down into your root chakra at the base of your spine. This chakra is to be visualized as a swirling vortex of energy, red and orange in color. Perceive the reds and oranges, and feel the balancing and energizing that is taking place here. Opening, balancing, energizing.

(Pause for five seconds.)

And your chakras are opened, balanced, and charged, thus expanding your aura and attuning you to the subtle vibrations that support the perception of subjective awareness.

And it's now time to imagine the bright white light moving back up into heart area. Visualize your heart center overflowing with the Universal light of life energy.

And now imagine the light emerging from your heart center to surround your body in a protective aura of bright white God light.

And you are totally protected. Totally protected. Only your own Guides and Masters or highly evolved and loving entities who mean you well will be able to influence you in any way in this altered state of consciousness session.

And as you continue to focus upon the sound of my voice, I am going to count you down, down, down . . . so vividly imagine yourself in a situation going down . . . walking down stairs, downhill, down the side of a pyramid . . . or any situation in which you see yourself going down, while I count backwards from seven to one.

Number seven, deeper, deeper, deeper, down, down, down.

Number six, deeper, deeper, deeper, down, down, down.

Number five, deeper, deeper, deeper, down, down, down.

Number four, deeper, deeper, deeper, down, down, down.

Number three, deeper, deeper, deeper, down, down, down.

Number two, deeper, deeper, deeper, down, down, down.

Number one, deeper, deeper, deeper, down, down, down.

And you're relaxed and at ease, and you feel deep. But let's go down a little deeper now . . . deeper now.

Number seven, deeper, deeper, deeper, down, down, down.

Number six, deeper, deeper, deeper, down, down, down.

Number five, deeper, deeper, deeper, down, down, down.

Number four, deeper, deeper, deeper, down, down, down. Number three, deeper, deeper, deeper, down, down, down.

Number two, deeper, deeper, deeper, down, down, down.

Number one, deeper, deeper, deeper, down, down, down.

You are now relaxed and at ease, and a quietness of spirit fills your body and mind. And within the multilevels of your mind lies an awareness of everything that has ever happened to you throughout all time. On a Higher Self level, you're aware of how all the people in your current life relate to your past lives. You're also aware of time spent on the other side between lifetimes and of your Spirit Guides, who are even now assisting you in accomplishing the growth you desire.

Your primary Spirit Guide has been with you since birth, always assisting you to fulfill your personal mission. Love is the power behind the guidance.

And it's now time to make contact with your primary Spirit Guide so you may directly communicate anything you'd like to know about. You will begin by perceiving your Spirit Guide's name. There are many names in many languages, including all those you've never heard spoken. So do not prejudge what you receive. Simply allow the letters of your Guide's name to come into your mind, one letter at a time . . . so now, trust the first letter of your Guide's name to come in.

(Pause for ten seconds.)

The second letter . . .

(Pause for ten seconds.)

Third letter . . .

(Pause for ten seconds.)

Fourth letter . . .

(Pause for ten seconds.)

Fifth letter . . .

(Pause for ten seconds.)

And if there are additional letters, allow them to come in now . . .

(Pause for fifteen seconds.)

And you should now have your Guide's call name. Say it over and over, silently in your mind . . .

(Pause for eight seconds.)

All right, it's now time to perceive exactly what your Guide looks like. So on the count of three, he or she will mentally appear before you. You will trust your impressions as you have never trusted before.

Number one . . . you're opening and asking your Spirit Guide to appear before you. Number two . . . your Guide is preparing to manifest before your inner eyes. And number three . . . perceive your Guide before you.

(Pause for ten seconds.)

If necessary, allow your Guide's image to form one part at a time. Then explore whether they are appearing in male or female form . . . How old do they appear to be? . . . What about their hair color? . . . Perceive your Guide's attire. Allow the image to form.

(Pause for forty-five seconds.)

And you should know your Spirit Guide's name and have an idea what they look like . . . how they prefer to appear to you. And now, it's time to use thought language to communicate directly with your Guide. Ask questions in the form of thoughts, then perceive your answers in the form of returning thoughts. Find out if you have a Support Guide or if you're working with any Masters . . . Go ahead now, communicate with your Spirit Guide.

(Pause for six minutes.)

All right, it's time to let go of this, and unless you've already done so, ask your Guide about his or her past lives. Find out if the two of you have ever shared an incarnation. Let this awareness come in the form of visual impressions and thought language.

(Pause for five minutes.)

And it's time to let go of this. Remembering everything you perceive, now go ahead and discuss with your Guide the areas of your life that you most need to work on to fulfill your earthly purpose.

(Pause for three minutes.)

And again, let go of this. Remembering everything you're perceiving, but it's time to return to your waking world. So take a moment to thank your Guides for their assistance. And know that you can communicate with them any time you desire to do so.

(Pause for ten seconds.)

And in just a moment I'm going to wake you up. On the count of five, you will open your eyes and be wide awake, fully alert, thinking and acting with calm self-assurance. You'll awaken feeling as if you've just taken a relaxing nap, and you'll be at peace with yourself, the world, and everyone in it.

Number one, coming on up now and feeling an expanding spiritual light within.

Number two, coming up, feeling at peace with all life.

Number three, coming on up and tapping into an internal balance and harmony.

Number four, recall the situation in the room. And number five, wide awake, wide awake. Open your eyes and feel good. Number five, wide awake.

Spirit Guide/Earthly Purpose
Guided Meditation

You're breathing deeply and relaxing completely.

Breathing deeply and relaxing completely... and allowing a quietness of spirit to come in. Taking a deep breath in and holding it as long as you comfortably can ... then let the breath out slowly through slightly parted lips, and when the breath is all the way out, push it further out, and further out ... and then repeat the process. Breathing deeply, and when any outside thoughts come into your mind, simply brush them aside and tell yourself, "I'll deal with that later," and then return your concentration to the sound of my voice, and breathing deeply and relaxing completely.

And in just a moment I'm going to relax your body one part at a time. So play the role, play the part, and feel your body relaxing as I ask you to do so. And the relaxing power is coming into the toes of both of your feet at the same time ... and it's moving right on down into the balls of your feet, into your arches, into your heels, and right on up to your ankles. Completely relaxed, completely relaxed ... and the relaxing sensations now move on up your legs to your knees, relaxing all the muscles as it goes. And on up your legs now, to your thighs and to your hips. Permeating every cell and every atom.

And you're relaxing completely, relaxing completely, keeping your full attention on the sound of my voice and relaxing your body, as the relaxing sensations move on down into the fingers of both of your hands . . . relaxing your hands. Feel your hands relaxing. And your lower arms are relaxed, and your upper arms are relaxed. Fingers and hands and lower arms and upper arms . . . just completely relaxed.

And the relaxing sensations now move on down into the base of your spine, your root chakra. Imagine a warmth in your root chakra as if a ray of sunlight were coming into the room and falling upon your spine . . . and it feels good. You imagine this warmth now moving up your spine . . . up your spine . . . up your spine and into the back of your neck and shoulder muscles. And your shoulder muscles are now loose and limp . . . loose and limp . . . just completely relaxed. And the relaxing sensations now move on up the back of your neck and into your scalp. Relaxing your scalp. Feel your scalp relaxing, and feel the relaxing sensations now drain down into your facial muscles, relaxing your facial muscles. Your jaw is relaxed. Allow a little space between your teeth. And your throat is relaxed. Your entire body is now relaxed all over in every way. And all tension is gone from your body and mind.

And we're now going to balance and energize your aura and attune you to the subtle vibrations that support the perception of subjective awareness. So to begin, imagine a beam of iridescent white light coming down from above and entering your crown chakra of spirituality on the top of your head. Imagine the light . . . create it with the unlimited power of your mind. This is the Universal light of life energy, and you feel it stimulating this chakra center, which is purple in color. Visualize a swirling vortex of purple, and the light opens, balances, and charges this chakra center. Imagine the opening, balancing, charging.

(Pause for five seconds.)

And the light is now moving on down into the center of your forehead—your brow chakra, which is a swirling blue-violet vortex of energy. Perceive the blue-violet color, and feel the balancing and energizing that is taking place here. Opening, balancing, energizing.

(Pause for five seconds.)

And the light is now moving on down into your throat chakra, which is a swirling silvery-blue vortex of energy. Perceive the silvery-blue color, and feel the balancing and energizing that is taking place here. Opening, balancing, energizing.

(Pause for five seconds.)

And the light is now moving on down into your heart chakra, which is to be perceived as a golden glow. Perceive the golden color, and feel the balancing and energizing of your heart chakra center. Opening, balancing, energizing.

(Pause for five seconds.)

And the light is now moving on down into your solar plexus chakra, located at the level of your navel. This chakra is to be visualized as several shades of red in color.

Perceive the red colors, and imagine the balancing and energizing that is taking place here. Opening, balancing, energizing.

(Pause for five seconds.)

And the light is moving on down into your sacral or spleen chakra, which is located a little below your navel. This swirling vortex of energy is a rainbow of colors. Perceive the many colors and feel the balancing and energizing that is taking place here. Opening, balancing, energizing.

(Pause for five seconds.)

And the light is now moving on down into your root chakra at the base of your spine. This chakra is to be visualized as a swirling vortex of energy, red and orange in color. Perceive the reds and oranges, and feel the balancing and energizing that is taking place here. Opening, balancing, energizing.

(Pause for five seconds.)

And your chakras are opened, balanced, and charged, thus expanding your aura and attuning you to the subtle vibrations that support the perception of subjective awareness.

And it's now time to imagine the bright white light moving back up into heart area. Visualize your heart center overflowing with the Universal light of life energy.

And now imagine the light emerging from your heart center to surround your body in a protective aura of bright white God light.

And you are totally protected. Totally protected. Only your own Guides and Masters or highly evolved and loving entities who mean you well will be able to influence you in any way in this altered state of consciousness session.

And as you continue to focus upon the sound of my voice, I am going to count you down, down, down . . . so vividly imagine yourself in a situation going down . . . walking down stairs, downhill, down the side of a pyramid . . . or any situation in which you see yourself going down, while I count backwards from seven to one.

Number seven, deeper, deeper, deeper, down, down, down.

Number six, deeper, deeper, deeper, down, down, down.

Number five, deeper, deeper, deeper, down, down, down.

Number four, deeper, deeper, deeper, down, down, down.

Number three, deeper, deeper, deeper, down, down, down.

Number two, deeper, deeper, deeper, down, down, down. Number one, deeper, deeper, deeper, down, down, down.

And you're relaxed and at ease, and you feel deep. But let's go down a little deeper now . . . deeper now.

Number seven, deeper, deeper, deeper, down, down, down.

Number six, deeper, deeper, deeper, down, down, down.

Number five, deeper, deeper, deeper, down, down, down. Number four, deeper, deeper, deeper, down, down, down. Number three, deeper, deeper, deeper, down, down, down.

Number two, deeper, deeper, deeper, down, down, down.

Number one, deeper, deeper, deeper, down, down, down.

And you are now completely relaxed and at ease. It's now time to humbly request your Spirit Guide's loving assistance . . . so silently in your mind, repeat after me:

"I call out to my primary Spirit Guide . . . I ask your loving support and to guide me in attaining the wisdom to transcend restrictions . . . Guide me in fulfilling my earthly purpose, as long as your assistance does not conflict with my karma or spiritual laws . . . I seek a sacred connection, combining your energy with my own to help me understand and fulfill my earthly purpose . . . Please help me accomplish my goal . . . I sincerely thank you from the bottom of my heart for your support and assistance . . . I desire to become successful . . . I ask it, I beseech it, and I mark it, and so it is."

And now take a few moments to imagine the loving presence of your Spirit Guide.

(Pause for fifteen seconds.)

All right, let's begin to program the fulfillment of your goal to understand and fulfill your earthly purpose. We all have karma to resolve and dharma to fulfill. Your dharma is your duty to yourself and to society. It's a big part of your earthly purpose. In addition, your earthly purpose includes learning to let go of fear and to express unconditional love. Letting go of fear means all the fear-based emotions, such as prejudice, selfishness, possessiveness, greed, envy, insecurity, inhibitions, blame, resentment, repression, and fears, such as fear of commitment, intimacy, and abandonment.

Unconditional love is a matter of expressing compassion and accepting others as they are, without judgment, blame, exceptions, or manipulation.

And now let's begin with positive suggestions communicated to every level of your body and mind. You will accept and act upon them.

You now begin to fully understand your earthly purpose . . . your duty to yourself and society.

You obtain awareness in dreams and meditation.

You know that everything talks to you, and you watch for signs providing direction.

In seeking to fulfill your life's purpose, you open to Higher Guidance.

You are willing to do what you need to do to fulfill your quest.

You now combine your energy with your Spirit Guide's energy to focus your power. You do, and it works for you.

You consciously work to rise above your fear-based emotions.

Every day in every way, you become more clear on your intent.

You accept others as they are, without trying to change them.

You easily express compassion and let go of judgment and expectations.

You are ready, willing, and able to fulfill your earthy purpose.

And these suggestions have been communicated to every level of your body and mind, and they've been accepted on every level of your body and mind . . . and so it is.

And now, imagine what your Spirit Guide looks like, and visualize the two of you working together to help. You understand and fulfill your earthly purpose. Imagine the assistance you're receiving. As one example, perceive your-self accomplishing what you're here on earth to do. Just make it up if you're not yet clear, Then, each time you do this session, you'll know a little more about your purpose. Use this opportunity to explore potentials and make this fantasy real.

Be there.

(Pause for ninety seconds.)

And what you've imagined is real . . . your reality. Your Spirit Guide helps you to understand and fulfill your earthly purpose, including helping you to be more compassionate . . . to easily express unconditional love, while at the same time resolving your karmic need to rise above fearful emotions.

And it's now time to communicate your desires to every level of your body and mind . . . so say these words along with me, silently in your mind:

"With my Spirit Guide's help, I now come to understand and fulfill my earthly purpose."

(Say this ten times.)

This is true. You accept that with your Spirit Guide's help, you focus your energy upon understanding and ful-filling your earthly purpose. And you are willing to do what you need to do to fulfill this quest.

And it's now time to use visualization to see yourself already understanding and fulfilling your earthly purpose. Imagine yourself in a vivid fantasy, and perceive every detail. You're fulfilling your earthly purpose. Sense the spiritual satisfaction. Feel the accomplishment. You've done it . . . through imagery, you communicate your desire to your subconscious mind, which assists you by generating circumstances to match your inner programming to your external reality . . . so go ahead and visualize while I am quiet for a little while.

(Pause for ninety seconds.)

And you will remember everything you just experienced, and you will act upon any awareness that will assist you to fulfill your earthly purpose.

You now begin to fully understand your earthly purpose . . . your duty to yourself and society.

You obtain awareness in dreams and meditation.

You know that everything talks to you, and you watch for signs providing direction.

In seeking to fulfill your life's purpose, you open to Higher Guidance.

You are willing to do what you need to do to fulfill your quest.

You now combine your energy with your Spirit Guide's energy to focus your power. You do, and it works for you.

You consciously work to rise above your fear-based emotions.

Every day in every way, you become more clear on your intent.

You accept others as they are, without trying to change them.

You easily express compassion and let go of judgment and expectations.

You are ready, willing, and able to fulfill your earthy purpose.

And these suggestions have been communicated to every level of your body and mind, and they've been accepted on every level of your body and mind . . . and so it is.

All right, now before awakening, your Spirit Guide is going to send you a message. On the count of three, your Guide will project a thought to you. It will be the most important message you could hear at this time. So trust now. The words will come into your mind on the count of three.

Number one . . . number two . . . and number three.

(Pause for twenty-five seconds.)

And you will awaken in a few moments remembering this message and everything else you perceived in this session. But now focus your attention on your breathing once again . . . take a deep breath . . . and thank your Spirit Guide for the assistance you've received.

(Pause for ten seconds.)

And in just a moment I'm going to wake you up. On the count of five, you will open your eyes and be wide awake, fully alert, thinking and acting with calm self-assurance. You'll awaken feeling as if you've just taken a relaxing nap, and you'll be at peace with yourself, the world, and everyone in it.

Number one, coming on up now and feeling an expanding spiritual light within.

Number two, coming up feeling at peace with all life.

Number three, coming on up and tapping into an internal balance and harmony.

Number four, recall the situation in the room.

And number five, wide awake, wide awake. Open your eyes and feel good. Number five, wide awake.

Walk-Ins and Wanderers

Dick Sutphen brought the concept of walk-ins and wanderers to his seminar participants after many long discussions with friends, such as the author and journalist Ruth Montgomery, who was convinced that Dick was a walk-in. He described the concepts this way:

Millions of people don't feel as if they belong here on earth. Something within their psyches says that this is an alien place and their true home is elsewhere. Most never connect their deep sense of being different with a nonearthly origin.

These are people born of earthly parents who incarnated to fulfill an earthly purpose. People who feel this way seem to fall into two basic categories: *wanderers* and *walk-ins*.

Wanderers are souls who have incarnated from a more evolved civilization, with their memories of identity and origin blocked . . . just as memories of past lives are blocked until we investigate them with metaphysical techniques.

Wanderers volunteered for the purpose of serving humanity of a planet in need of help. This service may be subtle, or the wanderer may be destined to become a major influencer.

Once born, they are as ordinary as everyone else, so it takes real metaphysical effort for them to realize their true identity. If they don't remember, they can easily become entangled in earthly snares and never fulfill their plans.

Wanderers typically thought of themselves as odd as children, are overly sensitive, kind, gentle, peaceful, and nonaggressive. They are not interested in money and have a hard time recognizing evil and trickery. They cherish great ideals, have strong interest in metaphysics, feel somewhat alienated, and oftentimes have strong interests in UFOs.

Walk-ins are souls who participated in a "soul transfer" with another human being who wished to depart from the physical world without dying and without incurring additional karma. The departing soul often feels overpowered and incapable of handling life. Walk-ins step in for humanitarian purposes, choosing to clean up the problems the departing soul has. After the task is completed, the walk-in is free to pursue their own service agenda.

In the many years I have conducted this session, I have only come across one person that felt they are a walk-in. If you have these traits and tendencies, you are most likely a wanderer. This session is for you to explore if you are a wanderer or a walk-in . . . and if not, maybe you know someone who is.

Walk-In and Wanderer Session

You're breathing deeply and relaxing completely.

Breathing deeply and relaxing completely . . . and allowing a quietness of spirit to come in. Taking a deep breath in and holding it as long as you comfortably can . . . then let the breath out slowly through slightly parted lips, and when the breath is all the way out, push it further out, and further out . . . and then repeat the process. Breathing deeply, and when any outside thoughts come into your mind, simply brush them aside and tell yourself, "I'll deal with that later," and then return your concentration to the sound of my voice, and breathing deeply and relaxing completely. You are feeling relaxed and at ease, at peace with yourself, the world and everyone in it.

And I want you to imagine a bright light coming down from above and entering into your crown chakra. Now make this real, and visualize an iridescent, bright light filling your body with love and protection. And it's now time to imagine the bright white light moving into your heart area. Visualize your heart center overflowing with the Universal light of life energy. And now imagine the light emerging from your heart center to surround your body in a protective aura of bright white God light.

And you are totally protected. Totally protected. Only your own Guides and Masters or highly evolved and loving entities who mean you well will be able to influence you in any way in this altered state of consciousness session. And I want you to silently, in your mind, call out to your own Spirit Guide to come in and be with you in this session. So go ahead, call in your Spirit Guide.

(Pause for ten seconds.)

And your Guide is now here with you. So now, to begin this wanderer and walk-in probe, quiet your mind and allow the questions of spirit to come in. The goal of this session is to see if you are either a wanderer or a walk-in, and if you are, to better understand your origin and your earthly purpose. If you are neither, you can use this time to see if anyone you know is from elsewhere. So breathe deeply and relax completely. Breathe deeply and relax completely. Allow the quietness of spirit to fill your body and mind to overflowing with peace, light, and love.

(Pause for ten seconds.)

All right . . . you are now psychically open and receptive, and I'm going to ask a question, which you will immediately answer in your mind, yes or no. Just trust the answer that emerges from deep within your subconsciousness memory banks. Remember, your Spirit Guide is right beside you. OK . . . are you a wanderer or a walk-in, yes or no?

(Pause for five seconds.)

If you're not a wanderer or walk-in, on a superconscious level, do you know anyone who is? If so, allow their name to come into your mind, now.

(Pause for five seconds.)

All right . . . if you are a wanderer or walk-in, the following questions and explorations will apply directly to you. If you're not and know someone else who is, the questions will apply to the other person, with whom you now make a mental connection.

(Pause for five seconds.)

OK . . . are you a wanderer or a walk-in? Choose which.

(Pause for five seconds.)

All right . . . it's now time to perceive information about your background, your true identity and origin. Trust every thought, feeling, and visualization . . . and know that you can ask your own questions with thought language and then trust as your question is answered in the form of another thought or visualization. OK . . . I'll be quiet for several minutes while you explore on your own. Get ready to begin receiving on the count of three.

Number one, number two, and number three.

(Pause for four to five minutes.)

All right . . . let go of this now, remembering everything you've learned. Let's move on and explore your real reason for incarnating as a wanderer or walk-in. Explore your earthly purpose or the earthly purpose of the soul you know to be from elsewhere.

(Pause for four to five minutes.)

All right . . . let go of this, remembering everything you perceived in this metaphysical probe. You will awaken feeling as if you've just taken a nice, refreshing nap. Your head will be clear, and you'll be thinking and acting with calm self-assurance, feeling glad to be alive.

On the count of five, you will open your eyes and be wide awake, fully alert, thinking and acting with calm self-assurance. You'll awaken feeling as if you've just taken a relaxing nap, and you'll be at peace with yourself, the world, and everyone in it.

Number one, coming on up now and feeling an expanding spiritual light within.

Number two, coming up feeling at peace with all life.

Number three, coming on up and tapping into an internal balance and harmony.

Number four, recall the situation in the room.

And number five, wide awake, wide awake. Open your eyes and feel good. Number five, wide awake.

Walk of Life Meditation

I found this meditation in some of the many files my husband left me. He had a posted note stating, "This is a condensed version of one of my tape releases." This is one of several audio programs that has been lost over the years.

Close your eyes. Breathe deeply and relax completely.

Breathe through your nose and exhale through your mouth. Very deeply, very, very deeply . . . and feel calm and peaceful, relaxed and at ease . . . calm and peaceful, relaxed and at ease.

(Repeat the above one more time.)

And now imagine yourself outside in the country on a clear summer night. It feels good to be here. You feel safe and secure as you look up at the stars. You hear the sounds of the night . . . imagine this very, very vividly. Be there.

(Pause for forty-five seconds.)

It feels so good to be here, looking up at the stars and enjoying the night. And it's now time to draw down the Universal energy of the stars, so please imagine yourself drawing down the light . . . drawing down the energy of the stars . . . the positive powers of the universe . . . perceive this energy as being drawn down in the form of an illumination that enters your crown chakra on the top of your head . . . so do this now. Actually draw down the energy and allow it to become your reality.

(Softly.) The universal energy of the stars . . . draw down the light . . . the positive powers of the universe . . . the God light . . . the star light . . . the love light . . . let it happen . . . let it be . . . drawing down the universal energy of the stars . . . the light of the universe.

(Pause for forty-five seconds.)

And you are now filled with light, and you look to the eastern horizon to see the sky lightening, getting lighter and lighter . . . and as the sun rises, you offer thanks for all you have and all that you may become.

(Pause for forty-five seconds.)

And the sun is now above the horizon, and it feels warm on your skin . . . and you notice a trail off to your right. It's time to follow this trail . . . as it leads off into the forest. So go ahead and begin walking down the trail and into the trees . . . into the trees . . . into the trees . . . and you sense the coolness in the shadows, and you inhale the rich scent of the earth and foliage as you walk the path. The early morning dew is still damp on the grass, and sunlight flickers through the rustling tree leaves. And as you walk the path, you hear the birds and subtle sounds of the forest awakening.

(Pause for thirty seconds.)

And ahead of you, the path becomes brighter as you come to a clearing that borders a little river. Go ahead and step out into the clearing and notice an altar over by the water's edge. You are drawn to the altar, so go ahead and approach it . . . approach it. And as you get closer, you notice a gleaming and beautiful sword lying upon the altar. Sunlight glints on the blade . . . and you now notice the words carved upon the side of the altar. The words say, "The Sword of Mercy."

(Pause for ten seconds.)

And you feel compelled to kneel before the altar. So you kneel down, close your eyes, and imagine a swirling white light surrounding your body . . . surrounding your body . . . protecting you from all things seen and unseen, all forces and all elements.

(Pause for ten seconds.)

And now, as you stand up, you reach out and grasp the hilt of the sword . . . raising it slowly . . . and holding it before you . . . and it feels light and powerful in your hand as a vague feeling of peace begins to permeate your body and mind.

(Pause for thirty seconds.)

And for the first time, you notice a small boat tied to a tree by the water's edge. Examine the boat. It has a small rudder to steer with. And notice the river.

(Pause for ten seconds.)

And still carrying the Sword of Mercy, you feel compelled to get into the boat. So go ahead, get into the boat and untie it . . . that's it, get in and untie the boat, and use the rudder to steer out into the current of the river.

(Pause for ten seconds.)

And now as you drift on the current, you are moving into swifter, darker water . . . swifter, darker water . . . and you steer with one hand and grasp the Sword of Mercy with the other, as the boat careens downstream into the boiling turbulence . . . experience the turbulence and torque of your primary fears being reflected in the dark water. Look into the water, and see your fears. Look into the water, and see your fears.

(Pause for sixty seconds.)

And in your awareness of your fears, you suddenly realize that you have the power and ability to rise above the effect of your fears by choosing how you will view them. You suddenly understand that by resisting the fears, you give them power, so you raise the Sword of Mercy and point it at your fears . . . go ahead, raise the sword and point it at your fears, knowing wisdom and grace and mercy will calm the waters . . . feel the power of this sword of awareness and mercy . . . emanating forgiveness . . . feel the light flowing into your body and through your hands . . . into the sword and into your fears . . . feel the power . . . feel the power.

(Pause for sixty seconds.)

You notice a cottage off into the distance. The boat slides into shore, and you decide to approach the cottage. As you do, the door opens, and you're greeted by a white-haired woman with kindly eyes and a friendly smile. You sense that you can trust her, as she takes your hand and leads you into the cottage. So go with her . . . perceive the main room . . . the hearth, the crackling fire, the smell of wood smoke and freshly baked bread. Notice the table and chairs . . . the woman gestures for you to take a seat.

(Pause for ten seconds.)

Now watch as she crosses the room to retrieve a decorative wooden box from the shelf on the wall . . . returning to face you, she explains that within the box is an object that has meaning for you. The object relates to some purpose in your life . . . this could be in regard to a person, to your career, to a service, or anything else. What part of your life would you like to explore? Take a moment to consider.

(Pause for twenty seconds.)

All right, now reach into the box and withdraw the object and perceive it vividly in your hand . . . go ahead . . . take the object out, and perceive the importance of this symbol to you.

(Pause for sixty seconds.)

And know that you carry the Sword of Mercy within you and can draw upon this energy to rise above your fears . . . know, too, that by interpreting the symbols in your life, you expand your awareness and open to being all you can be.

And on the count of five, you will awaken filled with joy, at peace with yourself, the world, and everyone in it, and retaining the awareness you experienced in this peaceful meditation.

Number one, coming on up and remembering everything

Number two, coming on up at peace with all life.

Number three, coming on up, feeling balance and harmony.

Number four, coming on up, recalling your environment.

Number five, wide awake, wide awake. Open your eyes and feel good. Number five, wide awake.

About the Authors

Roberta Sutphen was married to and worked alongside her beloved husband, Dick Sutphen, for over a decade before he passed away in his sleep on the morning of September 1, 2020. Although he is in Spirit, he is still very much involved in Roberta's life and looked over her shoulder as she put together this book.

Dick Sutphen spent over fifty years researching human-potential and psychic abilities. He was known as "America's Leading Past-Life Therapist" by the Body Mind Spirit Festivals in England and Australia. As a specialist in Past-Life Regression and Spirit-Contact Therapy®, he had a private hypnotherapy practice, and was the first to mass-produce audio and video programs.

Dick created and conducted Master of Life, Bushido, and other Psychic and Reincarnation Seminars worldwide and developed innovative group hypnosis exploration techniques that are now being used internationally. Over a half million people have attended Dick's seminars.

As a professional hypnotherapist, he was well known for his hypnotist trainings and received numerous awards.

Between 1976 and 2012, Dick wrote, produced, and recorded over 900 audio and video programs, which included hypnosis, meditations, sleep programming, and audio books. Most were released by Valley of the Sun Publishing, but he also created projects for several other audio publishers. Currently Hay House and the Numero Group own the rights to Dick's audio programs and music.

Dick was an amazing man who gave us so much wisdom over a fifty-year career. This book is for all of Dick's students, seminar participants, and anyone in the hypnosis field who want to experience the words of a Master.

In peace and light,
Roberta Sutphen

Printed in the USA
CPSIA information can be obtained
at www.ICGtesting.com
JSHW011358061123
51534JS00013B/110